D0065179

Crying Wind

by
Crying Wind

MOODY PRESS
CHICAGO

ISBN: 0-8024-1676-4

Printed in the United States of America

Chapter One

Moccasined feet moved quietly down the dry arroyo. The only sound was that of leather fringe flapping against bronze skin.

Thunder growled in the distance, and a few flashes of lightning outlined the ragged, purple clouds as I began slowly to work my way up the sharp rocks of the cliff. My hands were already scratched and skinned from clutching at rocks in the darkness. I tried not to think about what would happen if I grabbed a loose rock or lost my balance. I knew only too well it would be a long and painful slide down the steep, granite hill with yucca spikes slashing at my legs.

Straining my eyes, I tried to see the narrow, almost invisible path that led to the secret circle on top of this sacred hill. I wondered if there had ever been such a dark night. A flash of lightning lit the hillside long enough for me to see the large rocks ahead. I was nearly at the top.

I felt dizzy, and my hands began to shake from hunger. I hadn't had anything to eat or drink all day. I had fasted to prove myself worthy to speak to my god.

In a few more minutes I would be talking to my god, Niyol, the great and mighty wind god of the Indians.

At last I reached the crest of the hill, and I hurried over to a flat stone buried in the earth. I knew that hundreds of other Indians had stood on this same stone in the distant past to call to their gods for help.

I carefully removed the feathers and stick from my leather pouch and tied them together with strips of rawhide. Then I drew our clan sign in the dust and stood to face the wind.

I stood to face the wind.

6

"Oh, strong and fearful wind, most powerful of all the gods, hear my words—"

I finished my prayer and threw my prayer stick into the wind and quickly turned my back, because to see your prayer stick fall to earth meant your prayer would not be answered. I hoped the wind would catch my prayer stick and blow it up into the sky.

The thunder warned me one last time to come down off the mountain before he let loose his storm horses. I quickly ran my hands through the dust to wipe out all traces of the drawing. Even as I did so the sky began to cry, and large, heavy drops of rain hit the tops of my hands and turned the dust on my fingers to mud.

I hurried across the open space to the large boulders that marked the path leading back down the hill. The drops of rain were bigger, and they stung when they hit my face. A loud clap of thunder crashed all around me and made me jump with fright. My buckskin dress was already becoming wet and heavy, and it clung to me, making it even harder to inch my way down the narrow path. I wondered if lightning would strike me as I hung to the side of the hill and if I would be found dead tomorrow.

My heart raced faster. I couldn't tell if I shivered from the cold rain or from fear or if I just trembled from hunger. I was nearly at the bottom when the gravel, loosened by the downpour, gave way under my feet. I slid the rest of the way down the hill. When I was sure I hadn't been hurt, I picked myself up and brushed off the mud and thanked Niyol for sparing my life. After all, he could have told the lightning to strike me, or he could have killed me from the fall. Wasn't the fact that he spared me a good sign? Didn't it prove I was in his favor? Perhaps it even meant he had heard my prayer.

After I got home I hung up my dress to dry out. It was heavy and sagging from the water it had soaked up. The elk-skin dress weighed sixteen pounds when it was dry, but now that it was wet it must weigh twice that much. Some of the beads on the right sleeve were missing. They would have to be replaced before I could wear it again. My moccasins would have to be cleaned tonight. If I left the mud on, they would be too stiff to wear by morning.

My body ached as I finally crawled into bed. My hands burned where they had been scratched raw. I was still hungry, but I couldn't eat until morning.

"Oh, well, it was all worth it if the wind heard my prayer—if—if—" I tried to ignore the uneasy feeling in the pit of my stomach and tell myself it was only hunger. I would eat a big breakfast tomorrow morning, and the empty feeling would go away.

The last thing I remembered before I fell into an exhausted sleep was, "If he heard my prayer, if—if—"

I was glad I believed in the wind god. He was the most powerful of all the Indian gods. The bear god was strong, but he slept all winter. I didn't want a god who was asleep half the year. The snake and horned toad were ugly gods. I didn't like them. The wolf and eagle were beautiful and clever, but they could both be killed, and you could see their bones turning white in the sun. The sun god was mighty, but you couldn't call on him at night, and during the day, clouds could cover his face. No, the wind god was the best. He could be everywhere. He couldn't be caught or killed. He could blow your house down. He could tear at you until you couldn't stand up against him. He could be so cold he could freeze you to death or so hot that you would faint from his hot breath. Of course, the wind was a fickle god; he could be good or evil; he could answer your call or not, as he chose. But a god can't be everything. A god can't be perfect, and I was satisfied with this one.

It was Grandmother who had taught me all about the Indian

8

gods and legends. I had been with her ever since I could remember, ever since my mother had abandoned me.

I was never really sure why she took me in when my mother left me behind. Grandmother had had seven sons and four daughters, and certainly didn't need another mouth to feed. I knew she was disappointed because I was a girl. In our culture sons meant everything, and a daughter was practically worthless. Whenever a girl was born, people would shake their heads sadly and say, "Don't feel bad, maybe the next time you will be lucky and have a son."

After a few years had passed, I was big enough to help with the cooking and cleaning and any other work that was considered too lowly for my uncles to do. I learned to do "woman's work"— chopping wood, skinning the animals my uncles killed for meat, gardening, and feeding the livestock. I was too skinny to be very much help, and many times I failed to do things because I wasn't strong enough. My grandmother would shake her head, throw her hands up in the air, and say, "You are lazy! You are lazy!" Then she would scratch my arms with her fingernails until they bled to let the lazy blood out of my body so I could work harder.

Grandfather had died when I was small, and gradually my aunts had married and left home. My uncles had drifted away, one by one, until there was only Grandmother and me left in the little house.

Grandmother's face had a thousand wrinkles and looked like old leather. Her eyes were black and sharp as an eagle's beneath her hooded eyelids. Her hair was as white as snow, and she wore it in two braids. When she was a young woman, she had been beautiful. Her hair had been black and shiny and had hung past her hips. When Grandfather had died, she had cut off her hair to show she was in mourning. She had taken a knife and cut the palms of her hands to show her grief. In the old days Indian women often cut off their fingers when they lost their husbands.

9

Now her hands were wrinkled and scarred and her left thumb had been injured so that the thumbnail was always split down the middle, but her fingers were nimble for a woman her age, and she could do finer beadwork than any other woman in the valley.

Grandmother. *Shima Sani*—"Little Grandmother," we called her. She looked a hundred years old. She wasn't sure, but she thought she must be in her eighties. Of course, even if she had known exactly how old she was, she wouldn't have said so, because there was always the danger that the Spirit Horse would hear her and say, "I did not know you had lived so long. It is past time for you to die." And he would take her away. Most of the older Indians would say, "I am 104 years old." That seemed to be a favorite number to say, but it was unlikely that any of them were much over 90.

Shima Sani was orphaned when she was a small child and had worked in other people's cornfields to earn enough money to keep herself and her two sisters from starving. When she was about fourteen, a laughing young Navajo man came riding by on the most beautiful black horse she had ever seen. He didn't even speak to her, but a month later he came carrying a shawl for her and a cigar box half full of nickels for her sisters. She married him a week later and followed him to his small farm in Colorado, where he, too, raised corn. There they had eleven children.

I couldn't remember Grandfather very well since he had died when I was still small. I could only remember his dark, tough skin and his loud, happy laugh and his whiskey smell. He was walking home from town one night, after spending his entire week's wages on liquor, and he passed out. The next morning his son Cloud found him frozen to death in a cornfield less than a quarter of a mile from our house.

I knew none of my uncles grieved for their father. He had

Cloud was the youngest of my uncles, he was the tallest and strongest.

11

beaten them too many times in his drunken rages and had nearly killed some of them. Once he had broken Pascal's arm.

Although Cloud was the youngest of my uncles, he was the tallest and the strongest. When he walked through the door of our house, he seemed to block the whole doorway. His head would touch the top of the door entrance, and his shoulders would almost touch each side.

No one was as big or as important in my life as Cloud. It was always an event when he came to the house. I looked forward to seeing him because he always livened things up with a story. Somehow he could take the most common, ordinary happening and tell it in such a way that would make it seem like an adventure. He was my idol. I thought no one in the world could be as strong or as handsome as Cloud. He could follow animal tracks no one else could find and tell you within an hour when the animal had passed through. No wonder he was the best hunter and trapper around.

My uncle Flint was as tall as Cloud, but he was thin and didn't have the weight or strength that Cloud had. He was quiet and moody and never joked or laughed the way his brothers did. I wanted to feel close to Flint, but he always withdrew whenever I tried to be friendly, until I finally gave up and accepted the fact that Flint and I would never be close. We would always be strangers.

Pascal was several years older than Cloud and Flint. He had a sad face with deep lines around his mouth and a crooked wrist that hadn't been set right after Grandfather had broken his arm years ago. He was a quiet man—too quiet. You could never tell what he was thinking.

Once Shima Sani had tried sending me to the school in town, but it was a disaster. The other children in my class were all non-Indians and had made fun of my name, Crying Wind. They called me "Bawlin' Breeze." There are few things more precious

12

to an Indian than his name, and their jokes hurt me deeply. They had called me a wild savage and laughed at the beads I wore in my braided hair.

"Indians eat dog meat," they would call after me. "Hide your dog, or Bawlin' Breeze will eat it for supper—eat it raw!"

A few times I tried to tell them that if a person were starving to death he would eat anything to survive. Besides, Indian dogs weren't pets. They weren't the pampered, useless, spoiled things dogs are now. They carried small travois loaded with clay pots and blankets. They were watchdogs for the camp. When there was no game to hunt or when there were blizzards and the snow was too deep for the men to go hunting for meat, the dogs were already there in the camp and could easily be caught. Dog stew saved many people from starving in hard winters. Perhaps, when all was said and done, the Indians thought more highly of the dog than the white man, because the Indian's life often depended on his dogs.

I tried to tell them we weren't savages. It was the Indians who taught the white settlers about foods like jerky, popcorn, maple syrup, peanuts, corn, potatoes, rice, fruits, berries, and nuts. The Indians even had chewing gum hundreds of years ago. Most of the food the early settlers had was a result of the Indians' teaching them how to hunt, what to plant, and how to prepare what they caught and grew. But they never listened to me. They didn't care about history or facts; they only cared about having someone to laugh at.

I ran home in tears day after day while the other kids chased me, throwing rocks at me and calling me names. Finally, one day I decided I wouldn't take anymore. Instead of running, I stood my ground and put up a fight. It was a short one because one of the larger boys picked up a long stick and hit me across the mouth.

Blood gushed out and I was sure he'd knocked out every tooth

13

I owned. The sight of blood sent panic through the small mob, and they turned and ran, leaving me alone in the schoolyard with a swollen mouth and blood dripping off my chin, onto my only dress.

I ran all the way home. Grandmother had seen me coming and was waiting at the door for me.

I told her what had happened as she wiped away the blood and changed my clothes.

I was relieved to learn I only had a split lip and cut gums and that none of my teeth had been knocked out. My mouth was so sore and swollen I couldn't eat or talk for a couple of days. I enjoyed being petted and pampered by Grandmother and my uncles, who were furious at the way I'd been treated and called my attackers a pack of yellow dogs.

Cloud had been so angry he'd gone to the schoolhouse to talk to the teacher, But she wasn't interested in our problems. She said her job was to instruct the children in the classroom from 9:00 A.M. to 4:00 P.M., and anything that happened to a pupil after 4:00 on the way home was none of her business.

Cloud had come home with his temper blazing. "White man's schools!" he spat. "Let them be for the white man's children! Cry will not return!"

Grandmother nodded in agreement.

I could have shouted for joy. I would never have to return to that daily torture they called school. No more being taunted or chased or beaten up! No more angry looks from teachers. No more pointing fingers and laughter from the children.

True to my uncle's words, I never returned to school. Grandmother received several letters from the school demanding that I return, but she just threw them into the fire and never bothered to answer any of them. Once some people came out in a big fancy car, but Grandmother met them in the yard and spoke to them while I hid inside the house. I don't know what she said

14

to them, but they never returned, and the subject of school never came up again.

Grandmother gave me the proper education for a girl of my age. I was taught how to skin animals and tan their hides, how to do beadwork, and how to make medicine from plants. During these long days of tedious chores she would tell and retell the stories of the glorious days when the Kickapoo were the "Lords of the Plains."

"In the old days—" she would begin, and I would listen carefully, anxious not to miss a single word of the exciting accounts of our tribe's past history.

Over and over she would say, "Kickapoo is a name to be proud of. Our real name is *Kiwigapawa*. It means, 'He moves about,' because our people were always restless, always looking for a home and never finding one. We were always searching."

I would feel a pang of anger as I remembered how the people made fun of the word *Kickapoo* as if it were some kind of a joke. They would say "Kickapoo" and laugh. They knew nothing about the honor or meaning of our tribal name.

Grandmother's voice would go on, "Our people fought everyone. There was not a tribe anywhere that did not fear the name Kickapoo. There were no better warriors than ours. We fought the Sioux, the Iroquois, the Fox, Chickasaw, Creek, the Osage, the Cherokee— we fought all those tribes and we always won. The Fox and Illinois Indians." She would laugh, "We wiped them from the face of the earth. Our people fought the French, the British, and the Spanish and drove the traders from our lands. We killed the missionaries and burned their churches." Her eyes would snap with fierce pride. "There was no one who could win over the Kickapoo. Our warriors didn't think the odds were fair unless they were six to one against us. People's hearts stopped with fear when our name was spoken. From Maine to Mexico, our warriors left a bloody path."

15

She told me some of the stories about the great battles dozens of times, but I never grew tired of hearing them. Perhaps other children went to bed with stories or nursery rhymes, but I went to bed hearing about blood-chilling raids of the Kickapoo warriors. My heart would pound with pride at the stories of our past victories against our enemies and burn with anger at the stories of the lies and broken treaties thrown at us from the government.

Grandmother loved telling stories about Kennekuk, who was called "the prophet." Kennekuk had started a new religion among the Kickapoo in 1830. Although it wasn't the old Indian religion, neither was it Christianity; but it was enough of both to keep the "new white man's religion" from getting started in the tribe.

Kennekuk died from smallpox about 1850. Before he died, he promised he would rise from the dead and come back to life in three days. His body was buried in a dry well, and a large group of his followers waited beside his grave for his last prophecy to come true. At the end of the three days many left, but some stayed on a few more days. More left each day until finally everyone was gone, and the body of the prophet remained at the bottom of the old, dry well on the dusty Kansas plains. Grandmother would always add, "But who knows, the prophet may return some day."

She told me about the battle of Bad Axe and the Black Hawk War and the battles of Dove Creek and Rush Springs. She told me about Chief Keotuk, Chief Kapioma, Chief Ockquanocasey, Chief Quaquapoqua, and Chief Wahnahkethahah. Names like Whirling Thunder, Little Deer, White Horse, and Big Elk would echo in my head as I pictured them swooping down on their enemies, killing them and galloping away with enemy scalps and stolen horses.

Time seemed to stand still on the reservation. One day was

16

so much like the next we didn't bother to keep track of the months, only the seasons. I knew before I got out of bed that each day was the same, yesterday, today, tomorrow, always the same. Only a birth or death in the family would change the monotony.

When one of my aunts became pregnant, everyone was over-joyed that there would be new blood in the family—but the happiness turned to tragedy when twins were born. It was a bad omen to have twins, because everyone knew that a woman was to have only one child, and the second child was an evil spirit that was following the first from the darkness before birth. The second baby lived only a few days. It became weaker and weaker, and then it died. The first baby thrived and grew strong and fat. My aunt told everyone that she just hadn't had enough milk for the second baby. I had never seen a set of twins on the reserva-tion. Something always happened to the second baby, but no one spoke about it. Some things were better left unsaid. People on the reservation understood how things must be and the Indian agent and other authorities couldn't be bothered—so another Indian lost one of her newborn babies—who cares?

I knew that there must be dark, shadowy things, bad things that Grandmother and my uncles talked about when I was sup-posed to be asleep, but I didn't know what they were. Even though I was curious, I wasn't sure I really wanted to know everything that went on around the reservation.

I was about ten years old when one of the dark facts burst into my life and left its shadow on me for years to come.

Grandmother and I had been asleep for hours when suddenly there was a wild, frantic pounding on our door. Grandmother got up to open it while I snuggled farther down into the blankets, too sleepy to care what was happening. Then I heard loud, excited talking. I could tell by the way Grandmother spoke that she was upset. I got out of bed, sneaked over, hid behind her, and I peeked around her long flowing nightgown. I was shocked at what I saw.

There in the darkness stood a young man, naked except for a loincloth of coyote skin. He was covered with mud and so terrified, he was shaking from head to foot.

He was begging grandmother for help. He said he had just gotten married and moved into the far end of the valley. He had been married only one month when his new bride died of pneumonia. He was grief-stricken and went to the medicine man for help. The medicine man had told him he could raise the young girl from her grave and make her live again. The young man had followed the medicine man's instructions to the last detail. He had stripped and covered himself with mud, and when the full moon had risen, he had gone to his wife's grave and covered it with the skin of a coyote. He had sat there for an hour, for two hours, and nothing happened. In the third hour the grave began to shake, the ground began to tremble, and he knew something evil was happening. This thing that was coming from the grave couldn't be his beautiful, sweet wife; it had to be something so terrifying that his mind couldn't grasp it. He jumped up from the grave, and clutching the coyote skin around his naked loins, he had run screaming through the night. He was afraid to stop, afraid to look back. I don't know how many houses he stopped at before he reached ours that night. He had been running a long way, because his body was streaked with sweat, and he was gasping for every breath. Suddenly he started screaming and turned around and ran off into the darkness.

"What's happening, Shima Sani?" I whispered as I watched the man disappear.

"He shouldn't have done that," she said quietly and shut and bolted the door.

I wasn't sure what she meant and what he shouldn't have

18

done, but I didn't think I wanted to know any more about it, so I followed her back to bed without saying anymore.

I felt cold and I started to put my arm around her to keep warmer but as soon as I barely touched her she jerked away quickly and asked, "What's that!"

"It's me, Grandmother. I am cold."

She tucked the blankets around me.

"What did you think it was?" I asked.

She waited a long time before she answered. "Maybe I thought it was a bug."

I laughed, knowing she couldn't have thought it was a bug. I was too young to understand the depths of her fear.

The next day the story was all over the countryside. The young man had gone to my uncle's house.

"He said he felt something coming out of the grave—he said he didn't know what it was, but he felt something and the ground was moving." The story was repeated over and over. Could it have been his wife? Maybe it had been evil spirits? Could the medicine man really raise people from the dead? What had happened to the young man? No one knew. Many people had seen him running through the night with the coyote skin flapping behind him, but no one knew where he had gone. We never saw him again; he never returned to our valley. No one ever moved into his house, and no one ever went to see if the grave of his wife had been disturbed. But no one ever quite forgot the story. Maybe a year or more would go by without hearing it. Then a group of people would discuss something they didn't understand or something they feared, and someone would begin, "I remember this one time—" and the story would be told again. The people would nod their heads. Some of the women would shiver and some would say it wasn't the earth he had felt tremble, it was himself, because he was so afraid. Others

19

would say that maybe the medicine man really could raise a person from the dead. Nothing was ever solved. No one ever knew what happened to the young man, and after discussing it awhile, everyone would shrug his shoulders and shake his head, and it would be forgotten again. For a while.

Chapter Two

Summers turned into winters and winters back into summers again. It was late August, and already the leaves on the trees spoke in dry whispers, warning of an early autumn. The wild asters made the valley deep purple, and the last of the loco weed was fading away. The songs of grasshoppers filled the air all day long as if they were trying to warn each other that summer was nearly over; perhaps even tomorrow the first frost could come.

I gathered more wood and stacked it beside a large tree. Later I would carry it back to the house, but right now I needed to catch my breath. I was hot and tired and needed a drink of water. I'd been gathering wood since early morning. I knew we would need it this winter, but right now, on this hot summer day, winter fires seemed far away.

I sank to the ground and lay flat against the earth with the grass tickling my face. I could feel my strength returning slowly, but I wasn't anxious to pick up any more wood, so I just rolled over on my back and watched the white clouds float across the turquoise sky.

The wind cooled me with his breath, and it felt good to be alive. It was late in the afternoon when I walked back toward the house.

When the house came into view I was surprised to see an old, blue pickup truck drive into the yard. Two women and a man got out of it and walked toward the house. One of the women had her face buried in her hands, and I could tell she was crying.

Grandmother hurried outside to meet them and put her hand on the shoulder of the crying woman.

I was too far away to hear what they said, but I felt it must be something very important, because Grandmother looked very serious. The man had a dark look on his face, and the other woman began to cry.

I walked slowly up beside the house. My curiosity was gnawing at me, but I knew better than to interrupt, so I stood there motionless and waited.

After they had talked a few more minutes, Grandmother turned back up the path and went inside the house. A moment later she came back carrying an old quilt in her arms. She handed it to the man, who took it to the truck and wrapped it around something in the back. When he had finished he climbed into the truck and started the engine. The two women, still crying, got back into the truck with him.

I walked over and stood beside Grandmother but didn't take my eyes off the truck.

"Who are they? What did they want?" I asked, knowing they couldn't hear me over all the noise their old truck was making.

"They are Navajo. They live down on the flats. They used to know your grandfather," she said.

"Why did you give them a quilt?" I urged her on.

"They had a death in the family. They needed a quilt to wrap him in," she said.

Just then the truck backed up and pulled away and, for an instant, I saw the small bundle in the back of the truck.

"Is that—is that the body?" I already knew the answer, and added, "It's terrible for a little child to die."

"It wasn't a child. It was a very old man," Grandmother said, squinting to see the truck which was now nearly out of sight.

"But the body—it looked so small—"

"Yes, it was old Twice Blind, their medicine man. He died

22

angry and cursing, and his family was afraid he would walk back from the grave and haunt them. So they cut off his legs and buried them separately. Now they will bury his body far from home. They will make sure he cannot walk back from the grave."

The truck was gone, but Grandmother still squinted at the distance as if she could still see far beyond the horizon. "Old Twice Blind was a bad medicine man. He was always putting a curse on someone and making them pay him many sheep to remove the curse. Maybe now they will have a good medicine man."

I finished my work and went to bed, but that night I didn't sleep well. I had bad dreams about a small bundle in a quilt in the back of an old truck and about an old medicine man crawling around on his hands looking for his missing legs. That dream came back many nights, and I would wake up trembling and terrified. I wondered if it was really possible for Twice Blind to come back from the grave. I hadn't thought much about death before, but now I spent a lot of time thinking about old Twice Blind.

No one ever talked about dying; it was bad luck. Talking about dying would make you weak and sick.

Many times I wanted to ask Grandmother questions about death, but I was always afraid to bring up the subject. Then, one day while we were sitting together and quietly making beaded necklaces, I gathered all my courage and spoke so suddenly that I startled her. "Grandmother, what happens to us when we die?"

She looked up from her beadwork, and her hooded eyes looked like two pieces of black flint. "When you die, you die," she said simply and went back to her beads.

"No, Grandmother. I mean, what happens to us after we die?"

This time she did not bother to look up. "After you die, you are buried, and your body rots."

I swallowed hard. Was I pushing her too far? Would she become angry if I asked one more time?

"If your body rots, what happens to—" I didn't know the right word to use, "What happens to the rest of you—I mean your spirit?"

She looked up again, but she looked beyond me to somewhere in the past.

"I used to think there was a place the Great Spirit made just for Indians. It was a beautiful place where all the red people were always happy, and there was always plenty of food for everyone, and no one grew tired or old. Lodge fires never went out, and it was always summer." She was silent a long time, but I knew she hadn't finished. I waited.

At last she spoke again. "I used to ask the same questions you are asking now. I would say, 'How do we get to this place?' but no one ever told me. No one seemed to know. They would say, 'Ask the old ones.' I would ask them, but they would shake their heads and say, 'Our people used to know before the white man came, but we have forgotten and no one knows the way anymore.' Now I am old, and you ask me. I must say 'I do not know.' I am too old to live any more, and I am tired. I will be glad to die." And she added bitterly, "And to rot."

She looked again at her beadwork, but I caught a glimpse of something in her eyes. I knew I had to be wrong. It had looked like fear, but I knew my Grandmother was never afraid of anything. She would not be afraid to die when it was her time.

We finished the rest of our work in silence, and I was glad when I was allowed to go outside and be alone. I didn't like the answer she had given me.

So, I thought gloomily as I leaned on the corral fence, *so there is no place for the red man to go when we die. We rot.*

24

I watched an ant crawl along the top pole of the fence. "Are you and I the same? Am I not any better than a bug?" I took my fingers and brushed him to the ground. He landed unhurt and hurried along his way, but I didn't see him because my eyes were burning with tears. I remembered the look in Grandmother's eyes. I knew she was afraid, and that made me afraid. If death was something she couldn't face, then I knew I couldn't face it either. I felt as if the dark shadow had moved into my life again, and I wished I could move time backward to the days before I started to learn about life and death.

On hot, still, summer nights I could sometimes hear Cloud playing Indian songs on his wooden flute. The soft music would float down the valley to us like mist and then fade away. Not many of the young men knew how to play the ancient flute anymore, but Cloud did. He could play it better than anyone. In fact, he could do almost anything better than anyone I knew. I smiled as I wondered how many young girls wished Cloud would come to their homes and court them by playing his flute for them, but he never did. Many of the girls had tried to catch him, but it was beginning to look as if he would never be caught. Sometimes he would laugh and tease about the girls who would try to get his attention by leaving food on his doorstep or by just happening to be out riding their horses on the road when he was going to the trading post. He always made everyone laugh with his stories, but when he thought no one was looking, his smiling face became sober. His eyes had a lonely, far-away look. I wondered if he didn't really want to settle down, but he wanted someone besides one of the silly, young girls around here.

Sometimes Cloud would talk to me when we were alone, really talk to me as a friend and not just his niece or as a child. I always felt special when he spoke to me, like we'd shared a secret of some kind and that we were really alike in many ways.

Sometimes his music sounded so sad, I wondered if he felt dark shadows in his life, too. Someday I would ask him.

Autumn came late, but when she did come, she made up for it by being more beautiful than anyone could remember. Never had the leaves been such brilliant golds and reds. I spent hours just looking at the aspen trees on the hills around us. When I rode my horse, Thunder Hooves, through the piles of crunchy, dry leaves and watched them scatter beneath us, I felt strong and beautiful and wise, all the things I wasn't. The trees would drop their leaves down on me as I rode past as if to say "you are part of us, part of the trees and the earth and the wind." It was a good feeling, but it came to a sudden end.

An early snow came. It was a heavy, wet snow that piled up on the trees that hadn't yet shed their leaves, and it tore their limbs off. The golden leaves turned brown and black. The autumn beauty was gone forever, because there would never be another autumn as beautiful as that one was.

The snow came early and stayed and stayed. Months passed and the bare ground wasn't seen.

It seemed as if January would never end. Cold, gray clouds hung low over the mountains, and each day more snow fell from the sky. The wind was angry and slapped our faces and stung our hands whenever we had to go outside for more wood for the fire or to pump another bucket of water.

Grandmother complained of the cold and said her bones ached. She spent most of the time in her bed wrapped up in as many quilts as she could find.

"Don't worry, Grandmother," I would say as I piled more wood on the fire. "Spring will be here soon, and the sun will shine warm on us, and the snow and ice will melt, and the Mother Earth will breathe again. This spring I am going to get some seed from the store and plant bachelor's button flowers. I saw some in a woman's yard last summer, and they were bright blue and some were red. You'll like them, and they will make the yard look nice." I rubbed my raw, red hands together over the stove. "Spring will be here soon," I repeated.

"It had better hurry. I am old, and the winter makes me hurt. I get stiff, and it's hard to move," came her muffled voice from behind the pile of quilts.

"Would you like me to heat up the rabbit stew again? It might warm you up a little," I offered.

"Yes, I might like that," she said. She sat up for the first time since breakfast.

I carried the iron kettle over and put it on the heating stove. There wasn't much left so I added a little water to stretch it. I would have to walk down to Uncle Cloud's house and tell him we needed more food for tomorrow. I hoped he would have something besides rabbit. I was sick of rabbit stew. We had eaten it every meal for five days now.

Grandmother didn't seem to mind having it again, because she ate a large bowl of it and seemed to feel stronger afterwards. She got up and walked around the room and looked out the windows at the snow piling up everywhere.

The wind had grabbed the tar paper and tore it off and blew it away.

27

"Maybe spring won't come this year," she said as the wind made the windows rattle and blew more snow in through the cracks around the door.

"Spring always comes," I said.

"But maybe it won't come for me this year." She kept her back turned toward me.

"You'll see many springs come and go. This summer we'll fix the house up. We'll put in a better door, and your sons can patch the cracks in the walls to keep the cold out. Remember how much warmer it was last winter when he had the tar paper on the outside of the house before the wind tore it all off during that bad storm?"

She turned around and laughed, "The wind was jealous of our warm house, and when we didn't invite him inside, he grabbed the tar paper and tore it off and blew it away. Everyone was outside running around in the storm, trying to catch the pieces of tar paper, but they were torn into such tiny pieces they couldn't be used again."

She was getting in a better mood, and I wanted to keep her cheered up. "Well, this time we will nail it onto the house better, and the wind won't be able to take it away from us, no matter how hard he tries," I said boldly, hoping he wasn't listening and wouldn't punish me for defying him.

"It would cost twenty or maybe even thirty dollars to buy enough tar paper for our house. Where would we get that much money?" she shook her head.

"We can sell our beadwork at the trading post. If we start making things now, we might have enough by summer to buy what we need."

"Maybe," she agreed. "But when it's cold like this, my fingers are too stiff to do good work." She looked at her hands.

"My fingers aren't stiff. I can make a lot of things while it's snowing, and when spring comes and it's warm again, you can

28

sit in the sun and make bead necklaces. We could do it," I encouraged her.

It was getting dark. I would have to hurry if I was going to give hay to the horses and still have time to walk down to my uncle's house.

"I have to go do chores now," I told Grandmother. "I'll bring more wood in when I get back, so don't go outside yourself." I didn't have to worry. She was already climbing back under her quilts.

I pulled on my short, leather coat and tied a woolen scarf around my head. I could only find one glove, so I put it on and stuffed my other hand in my coat pocket. If I took time to look for the glove now I would be too late in getting to Cloud's house.

When I stepped outside the door a blast of cold air took my breath away and hurt my chest. My eyes stung from the freezing temperature, and I had to blink back tears as I hurried through the snow and toward the corral.

The sky was a pale pink in the west, and the snow looked pink where the sunset was reflected.

The horses saw me coming down the hill and lined up against the pole fence and whinnied at me. I pushed them aside as they crowded against me. Steam was rising from their backs. I could feel their body heat as I walked between them.

There was always a warm, horsey smell in the barn, and the air always seemed to be filled with dust and the scent of hay. The horses followed me inside, one by one. I knew War Cloud was the last one in, because he never picked up his left hind foot high enough to clear the board in the doorway, and he always kicked it.

They stirred around eagerly, and Thunder Hooves nipped War Cloud to make him move over and give her more room at the trough. I threw some hay over to them and stood there, watching them greedily munching. Thunder Hooves stopped chewing for a second and looked at me and then went back to her dinner. I decided to give them each a scoop of grain, even though there wasn't much left, and we had been saving it in case we ran out of hay. When they heard the oats being poured into their buckets, the horses nickered and stamped their feet. It wasn't often we had grain for them. They knew it was a special treat. I stroked Thunder Hooves's nose and patted her neck and reluctantly headed out of the barn, leaving the horses well fed and warm.

Thunder Hooves—was there ever a horse so beautiful? Her coat shone like morning sunshine, and her mane and tail were like white clouds. My Uncle Cloud had given Thunder Hooves to me when she was a foal. I could never be poor or alone as long as I owned such a fine horse.

First dust, months and months of hot dry dust, and then rain and mud, everything was mud, and now snow, so much snow.

Snow. I had almost missed it. I stuck my hand out and let the clean white flakes rest on my fingers. I looked at the tiny flakes. I had never really seen snow before, not so close. I'd never really paid any attention to it. Each flake, complex and perfect and beautiful. They say there are no two flakes alike. I reached out again and caught more snowflakes. They were so much like people, each one beautiful in its own design, each one different. Then the flakes began to melt and, in an instant, they were gone forever. Again, like people, here for an instant and then gone forever. Gone forever? Was that true? It was hard to imagine not existing somewhere, in some form. Perhaps people came back to live again as something else. Perhaps they even came back as snowflakes. If that were true, they would only come back for a short time and then be gone again. Was that what life was? Living and dying and then coming back to live and die again?

30

The snow no longer looked beautiful. I stuffed my hands into my pockets and ignored the snowflakes falling on my coat. I didn't want to look at them again. I didn't want to see how beautiful they were and watch that beauty disappear.

I walked down the valley and across the creek to my uncle's house. He was outside chopping wood. When he saw me, he put down his ax and came forward to meet me.

"Is anything wrong?" he asked.

"No, but I came to see if you have any food to spare. The rabbit you gave us will be gone by morning."

"I could get you a couple of chickens," he offered.

"That would be good for a change," I said. My mouth watered at the thought of fried chicken. "How's the trapping, Cloud?"

He shook his head. "No good. Snow's too deep, so I gave up and brought my trap lines in yesterday. This is not a good winter. I don't like it. Lots of bad luck. Yesterday I broke my knife. An Indian is no good without a knife. One of my traps fell into the stream and froze in the ice. I was trying to chip it out and broke the blade. That was a good knife. I've had it a long time. It will cost a lot to get another one that good; three, maybe four fox pelts. I'm going to the trading post tomorrow. Do you need anything?"

"Sugar, flour, and coffee," I said, "and some thread. I'm going to do some beadwork."

"The trader will be glad to hear that. He asked me last time I was in when you and Shima Sani would be doing more. He said he could sell a lot this summer." He looked at the sky. "You'd better leave now, or you won't get home before dark." He disappeared into his hen house. A few minutes later he came back with two chickens and tied their feet together so I could carry them back.

They were heavy and I stopped to change hands. This meant

31

laying the chickens in the snow, taking the glove off one hand, putting it on the other, picking up the chickens, and starting off again. I had to do that three times before I reached home.

I shut the chickens up in the woodshed. They would be all right there until morning. Then I took the hatchet and broke the ice on the water barrel and took a bucket of water inside. I made two more trips outside for wood. It was pitch black outside when I shut the door for the last time that night.

I had wanted to tell Grandmother we were having chicken tomorrow, but she was already asleep, so I lit a kerosene lamp and started a bead necklace. We wouldn't have to be cold next winter. We would have tar paper on our house to keep out the snow and wind.

I looked around me at the place we lived in and called home. It was only one room. One corner of the room was our "kitchen." A bucket of drinking water sat on the floor with a clean cloth spread over the top of the bucket to keep dust and bugs out. Some rough board shelves were our cupboards. The opposite corner of the room was our "bedroom," a lumpy, old double bed piled high with quilts and blankets. In the center of the room was a large, round table and five nonmatching chairs of wood, our "living room." Our clothes hung on wooden pegs near the bed, and an old wooden chest at the foot of the bed held a few personal belongings.

I was hungry, so I opened a can of evaporated milk, poured it over some bread, and added sugar. I wished I had remembered to put the can outside in the snow so it would have been cold. I liked cold milk, but since we didn't have a refrigerator or electricity, we couldn't have any foods that spoiled easily.

I watched Grandmother sleep and wished that somehow tomorrow could be different from all the hundreds of other days. Maybe I was restless because my fifteenth birthday was coming soon and something seemed to be missing from my life.

Several times lately Grandmother had reminded me that by the time she was fifteen, she had been married a year and had a child. Most of the other Indian girls my age were married, but I had never even had a date. The only men I ever saw or talked to were my seven uncles, who lived in the valley. Maybe when I was fifteen things would be different.

I put away my beadwork for the night. It was good to have something to do for a change. All my life I had had almost complete freedom to do anything I wanted to do, but it hadn't taken long to learn that freedom meant nothing to do, no place to go, no one to care. Soon things would change, because I would be fifteen. I would be a woman!

Chapter Three

I quietly slipped out of bed and into my clothes and hurried outside to meet the morning. It was going to be a wonderful day, because today I was fifteen years old. I was no longer a child; I was a woman. I would have new status in everyone's eyes. I heard some birds start their morning songs in the trees on the hill.

"Sing a happy song for me, little bird!" I said, and suddenly my joy of the morning was lost. Why had I said "little bird"? That was my mother's name, Little Bird. I didn't want to think about her, but sometimes she crept into my thoughts like a shadow across the sun. She had been silent nearly all the time she had been with me. She had never forgiven me for being born. She couldn't look at me without remembering how much she hated my father. Her name was Little Bird, but after I was born she had insisted that everyone call her "Little Dead Bird," because she said now she was dead. She had never touched me. When I was an infant, she had refused to feed me. My grandmother had saved me from starving to death by pouring canned milk and coffee and bacon grease down my throat.

Then one day my mother left, and I never saw her again. No one knew where she had gone. She had just packed up and said good-bye to Grandmother and some of her brothers, and she was gone. I didn't care that she had left, because now there was no one to give me long, hard stares out of cold, dark eyes. Now I didn't have to feel guilty about being born. The family spoke about her less and less and finally, not at all.

I wondered if my mother remembered that fifteen years ago

"An old woman likes her coffee in the morning."

today she had brought a life into the world. Did she ever think
of me? Was she even alive? Was my father alive?

No, I wouldn't think sad thoughts today. Today was going to
be happy.

I heard Grandmother stirring around inside the house and
turned my back on the rising sun and went inside. I hoped she
would remember it was my birthday.

"Good morning, Grandmother." I smiled and searched her face for some sort of sign that she knew this was a special day.

"You forgot to make coffee," she said. She added some water to yesterday's coffee grounds and put the pot on the stove.

"I'm sorry," I said. I reached for a skillet to fry some eggs and squaw bread.

"An old woman likes her coffee in the morning," Grandmother complained and blinked her sleepy eyes.

I patted out the squaw bread and dropped it into the hot grease, watched it turn brown and then flipped it over and took it out. Grandmother stood beside me waiting for the coffee to boil.

I broke some eggs into the skillet. Grandmother reached across the skillet to get the coffee pot. The eggs popped some hot grease on her arm. She jerked her arm back, dropping the hot coffee pot on her right foot. The scalding hot coffee and grounds spilled over her bare feet, and she cried out and stepped backwards.

I stooped down and started to brush the hot grounds off her feet but she slapped me across the face. I jerked back.

"Get away!" she snapped. She finished wiping off her feet. She shuffled over to the bucket of water and poured several dippers of cool water over her feet and legs.

I stood there helpless, my cheek blazing where she had slapped me. Tears blurred my eyes. I turned my back on her and looked at the spoiled breakfast. The eggs had turned black, the squaw bread was soaked with spilled coffee, and the floor was covered with coffee grounds. I started to clean up the mess, glancing over at Grandmother. I hoped she would say something, but I already knew what was coming next—the familiar silent treatment. She used it on me every time I did anything to make her angry. It seemed to happen more and more often lately. She would go for days, or sometimes even a week at a time, without saying one word to me. She ignored me completely. Sometimes I could hold out for a day or two, pretending I didn't care whether she spoke to me, but eventually the silence would wear me down. I would apologize to her and ask her forgiveness so she would speak to me again.

Today, of all days, I didn't want to get the silent treatment. I decided the sooner I apologized, the sooner it would be over with.

"I'm sorry, Grandmother. If I had made the coffee when I got out of bed you wouldn't have had to make it, and you wouldn't have gotten burned. Does it hurt?" *Well, at least that much was over with,* I thought as I swept up the floor.

No answer. She was mad and was going to sulk awhile. How I hated the silence and being treated as if I didn't even exist! It was only a small dose of one of the worst punishments the Indians used. In the old days, when someone had brought such shame to his family or tribe that it could never be forgiven, that person was declared dead by the family. A death chant was sung, and often a grave was dug and the person's belongings buried in it. That person no longer existed. The family never mentioned him again. It was the worst shame that could be placed on a person. It was hardly ever used anymore, but sometimes Grandmother would give me a little dose of it just to remind me that she was still the head of the family.

Even though all eleven of her children had left home now and some of them were married, she was still in control, and if she snapped the reins, her family obeyed.

I knew her feet hurt and that she blamed me for it. She had forgotten my birthday, and now there was no point in mentioning it. The day was spoiled.

I went outside and sat on a tree stump. Then I saw the horses coming up the draw toward the barn. I jumped up and started down the hill to meet them. I would go for a ride. That always made me feel better.

I grabbed a bridle out of the barn and caught Thunder Hooves. I put the reins around her neck to hold her while I slipped the bit into her mouth.

She wasn't happy about going for a ride; she had become fat and lazy and spoiled. I glanced over my shoulder at the house. I didn't see Grandmother, but I decided not to take time to saddle Thunder Hooves. If Grandmother saw me, she might think of some work for me to do, and I wouldn't be able to go riding.

I swung onto Thunder Hoove's back and urged her toward the timber. I was in a hurry to get out of sight of the house and away from Grandmother's anger.

Thunder Hooves broke into a full run. The pounding hooves

Thunder Hooves broke into a full run.

38

seemed to catch the rhythm of my own heartbeat. The cold wind whipped around me and bit through my threadbare shirt.

Gray clouds moved across the sky as if they were following us, trying to darken our winding path across the valley. My palamino pony raced with her head low and outstretched, her mane and tail flowing in the wind. I bent low over her neck, and her mane slapped me in the face. I held onto the reins with one hand and tangled my fingers into her mane for a better grip. My knees dug into her sides. I hung on as she seemed to fly over the rough ground.

I could feel her heart pounding between my legs. She was getting hot, and foam was appearing on her neck. She didn't start to slow down until we had reached the top of the highest hill around. Then I jerked her to a sliding stop and spun her around to look back in the direction we had just come.

I leaned down and felt the sweaty neck that was quivering from the run. I slid off her back and felt my own legs shake as they hit the ground.

"We're both out of shape, old girl," I said and patted her nose. I turned her loose to graze, and I walked a few feet and sat down on a pile of large rocks. I'd start riding more often. I used to ride every day, but lately Grandmother always found work for me to do.

I took a deep breath. The air was clear and fresh and smelled like pine. I felt better. I was glad I had come for a ride. I heard Thunder Hooves snorting behind me and chomping grass. She was a good horse. She was spoiled and hard to manage sometimes, and she wasn't the fastest or the smartest. But she was the beautiful color of liquid sunshine, and she was mine. She wasn't just a horse—she was the best friend I had. It bothered me that she wasn't young anymore. My uncles kept telling me to trade her off and get a colt, but they only thought of her as a horse.

39

I sat there until time didn't exist.

They didn't understand she was my friend, and I didn't want to trade off a friend.

I sat there until time didn't exist. I dreamed impossible things. I thought about the past and worried about the future.

It wasn't until I noticed how silent it was that I was forced back to the present. I jumped to my feet and looked around. Thunder Hooves wasn't anywhere in sight. I had let her wander off while I was daydreaming.

"Oh, please don't let her have gone home!" I said, not knowing to whom I thought I was talking. I didn't want to walk the three miles back home, not today—especially not today.

I ran over the far edge of the hill searching everywhere for her. There! There she was in a small stand of aspen trees. I hurried to her and grabbed her loose reins. I surely wasn't going

40

to take a chance of losing her now! I jumped on her back and pulled her head up. She stomped her feet while I tried to make up my mind where to go. I didn't want to go back to the house yet. I wanted to ride over the ridge and down the other side, but that would take at least another hour. I looked at the sky. It was getting late. I still hesitated. If I didn't get back in time to cook dinner I would be in trouble, and I was already in enough trouble today. Thunder Hooves shook her head up and down and snorted impatiently that she was eager to go.

"All right, you win." I headed her toward home but held her down to a walk. I wasn't in a hurry to get back. I felt as if this ride had been special. I didn't want it to end, because I felt like there would never be another ride quite like this one.

"Hey Thunder Hooves," I said. "Today is my birthday." Her head jerked up and down as if she understood.

We were both tired by the time we reached the barn. I slid off her back and took off her bridle. She sank to her knees and rolled over on her back, kicking all four feet into the air, and wiggled until she had rolled all the way over. Then she stood up and shook the dust off.

"You are only worth ten dollars, because you only rolled over once," I told her. I went into the barn and poured out a small can of oats for her. She was chewing the first mouthful before I stepped out the door.

I made my way up to the house. It was already getting dark, and Grandmother had lighted the kerosene lamps.

As soon as I stepped inside I smelled dinner cooking, and my heart sank. She was sure to be angry because I had stayed out so long.

I washed my hands in cold water and dried them on my shirt tail. "What do you want me to do?" I asked, and then added, "I went for a ride. I'm sorry I'm late." This seemed to be my day for apologizing.

"Food's ready," she said and spooned fried potatoes and deer meat onto a plate and handed it to me. Yellow grease ran off the potatoes and meat and covered the plate. She always cooked everything in the same skillet at the same time, so I knew the potatoes would have no taste of their own, only the wild taste of the deer meat.

She filled her own plate and sat down at the table. We ate in silence. When we were finished eating, she went over and sat on the bed and began mending an old dress.

I cleared off the table, dreading the long, silent night ahead of me when I heard a welcome noise. We could hear whooping and hollering long before they started up the narrow path that led to the house.

Grandmother's eyes shone with anticipation as she hurried to the door and flung it wide open. I stopped what I was doing and rushed to her side.

We knew from the rowdy noise that my uncles had gotten together and made another batch of trade whiskey. It was thick and black and the next thing to poison, but guaranteed to get a person rip-roaring drunk.

Five of them exploded through the door. We stepped aside to keep from being knocked down. Grandmother and I both laughed at their drunkenness. My uncles roared and shouted and staggered around the room, bumping into everything.

Flint and Cloud started shoving each other, and finally the two of them slammed into each other and went crashing to the floor in a heap of arms and legs and fists. They rolled around like two bear cubs in the spring.

Grandmother smiled indulgently. Her sons could do no wrong in her eyes. It didn't matter if they broke a little furniture or even if they tore down the house. They were young men; they needed to let off steam.

The two finally struggled to their feet. Flint gave Cloud a

hard shove and Cloud slammed into Flint with his shoulder. Flint spun around and came smashing into me, sending me hurtling backwards over a chair and up against the wall.

I doubled over in pain and couldn't breathe at all. The ache in my chest was almost unbearable.

Cloud and Flint each took an arm and dragged me to my feet and forced me to straighten up. Everyone was laughing.

"Got the wind knocked out of Crying Wind!" Grandmother said and reached for a bottle that was offered to her.

As soon as I had caught my breath, I was forgotten and left sitting on the bed in the corner of the room. My lungs still hurt. I had a bump on the back of my head. My elbows had been skinned raw when I had skidded across the wooden plank floor.

I kept smiling, and I laughed when anyone would say something funny, but I was hurting inside. It wasn't just the idea that when Flint had crashed into me I had taken a very hard fall and been hurt; that was an accident. What hurt most was that no one cared that I was hurt. I told myself I was being a spoiled child, and I should forget the burning tingle in my elbows and the throbbing headache and my sore rib cage. If I complained, everyone would laugh and make fun of me and call me a papoose.

I watched Grandmother as she accepted the drinks offered to her. She laughed at everything now and spoke almost entirely in Kickapoo. My uncles would argue and laugh and drink some more. They were all having a good time.

I faded into the dark shadows in my corner of the room. These were my blood relatives, my family. Why, why did I feel so left out and alone? Why did I feel as if a circle had been formed, and I had been left out? Was it because I was a girl, or was it because I was a half-breed? Why was it I never seemed to fit in anyplace?

All of my uncles got up and left except Pascal, and things

43

quieted down a little after the others had gone. The conversation was turning to more serious matters. Pascal seemed more eager to talk than usual and acted as if he didn't want to leave.

As the voices grew quieter, I pulled some quilts around me and turned my face to the wall. No one had remembered my birthday. No one was aware that, according to custom, I had become a woman today. I ached where my body had been hurt, but even more I ached where my heart had been hurt.

Pascal's voice could be heard far into the night, but I no longer heard his words or cared what he said. I only wanted to sleep and to forget this day.

Chapter Four

After my birthday I noticed that Shima Sani was limping, and I could tell she was in pain. We both pretended to ignore her trouble, but I was worried and knew she was, too.

She was getting worse all the time, and there could be no doubt that her feet hurt. It had been weeks since her feet were burned, and they had not healed. She spent as much time lying down as she could and avoided walking any farther than from her bed to the table to eat.

I had not seen her feet in a long time; she kept her tall moccasins laced up, and at night she wore heavy socks to bed.

Once when I came and caught her sitting in a chair, soaking her feet in a pan of egg whites, she told me to leave her alone. I went back outside to wait until she was finished. She had always used egg whites to draw poison out of an infected wound, so now I knew she had an infection in her feet.

She avoided talking about her feet, so I pretended not to notice how much trouble she was having getting around. I made sure I was outside at least an hour every afternoon in case she wanted to use her medicine without my seeing her.

At last she couldn't hide it any longer, and one morning she called me over to her bed. "My feet don't heal," she said. "I used all the old medicine I know. Nothing works."

I pulled back the covers on the bed, and as gently as I could, I began to unwrap the strips of cloth she had wound around her feet.

I had expected it to be bad, but nothing could ever have prepared me for what I saw.

45

The stench was almost unbearable. The rotten flesh hung loose around her toes. The skin was deep blue and green and black, and it was bloody. *Gangrene.* I gently wrapped some clean strips of cloth back around her feet, knowing there wasn't much time left.

"Grandmother—" I pleaded.

"No," she said flatly. "I know what it is, but I will have no doctor, no hospital, no one carving up my body. I won't wander forever, searching for lost pieces of my body. I will go to my grave as a whole person, just as I was born into this world a whole person. If I can't hold onto my life with my own two bare hands, I will let go of it."

We both knew she had just pronounced her own death sentence.

"Shall I go to my cave?" She smiled with a little twinkle in her eye.

"No, you don't need a cave, you have me," I said. She was remembering the old days, when an old person who had become useless and was a hardship or danger to the rest of the tribe would take a piece of jerky, a wad of tobacco, and a little water and sit in a cave and wait to die. It wasn't just considered a noble way to die; it was an obligation. No one person had the right to endanger the entire tribe. No one made the decision for you; it was yours and yours alone to make.

I went outside and threw the filthy rags into a ditch and set fire to them. I knew Grandmother had not been making a joke with me. She had been giving me a way out if I had wanted to take it.

I wouldn't let her die alone. I couldn't keep her from dying, but I could keep her from dying alone. I knew she was afraid. Maybe if I was with her when the end came she wouldn't be so afraid.

It was a dark day. Clouds had kept the sun covered, and I had overslept. When I finally did get out of bed, I was worried about it being so late in the morning, and I hurried around, making breakfast.

When the coffee was ready, I called Grandmother.

"Shima Sani, wake up. The sun slept late today, and so did we. Your coffee is ready."

She didn't move under the mound of quilts.

I walked over and put my hand on her shoulder. It was damp with sweat, and her skin was as hot as fire.

"Grandmother?"

Her eyes flickered open. They looked tired and dim. Her lips moved several times before any sound came. When she finally spoke, her voice was barely more than a whisper.

"Get Cloud," she breathed out. "I want my sons with me."

"What's wrong?" My voice trembled. "Grandmother!"

"I am not ready to die—I thought I was ready to die but I'm not—" Tears started to roll out of the corner of her eyes and across her wrinkled cheeks. "Get Cloud—get my sons!"

"I will. I'll run fast. Don't worry Grandmother, I will be right back with Cloud and the rest." I ran to the door and called over my shoulder, "Don't worry Grandmother, I will bring them right back!"

Thunder Hooves was standing in the corral. When she saw me running she must have sensed the urgency, because she edged toward the gate and stood still as I grabbed the bridle off the fence post and slipped it on her. I jumped on her bare back and kicked her hard with my heels. She leaped forward so fast, I nearly slid off her back. I grabbed a handful of mane with one hand and drove my heels into her ribs again. She was in a gallop before we passed the barn. As soon as we crossed the creek, I began hitting her with the reins. She laid her ears back and switched her tail and ran faster, faster than I had ever forced her to go

47

before, but it still seemed too slow. One mile. One mile to Cloud's cabin, but it seemed like a hundred. It could not have taken us more than a few minutes to reach the cabin, but it seemed like an hour. As soon as his cabin came into view I began screaming out his name.

"Cloud! Cloud!" I couldn't tell if my voice could be heard or if the wind was just whipping my words away.

I could see Cloud standing in the yard, throwing a knife at a fence post.

At last he heard my screaming and looked up. He began running toward me, and I yanked my horse to a sliding stop.

"Cloud!" I gasped. "Grandmother—something is wrong—she wants you now—she said she wanted all of her sons—"

"You go get Pascal. Tell him to meet me there." He took off his cowboy hat and hit Thunder Hooves on the rump. "Go!" he yelled, and we were off in a gallop.

Cloud ran for his truck. I heard the motor grind and the wheels spin as he headed for Grandmother. Thunder Hooves ran for another mile, but she was slowing down. Foam dripped from her mouth, and she was drenched with sweat. My jeans were soaked with her sweat and itchy from rubbing on her hair. My side began to ache from the constant pounding, and my legs were cramping from holding on. I had to slow down. There was still another mile to Pascal's cabin. I pulled her down to a fast walk. She snorted and shook her head up and down and stumbled several times. The pain in my side began to ease up, so I urged her back into a gallop for the next half mile.

I was in luck. Flint's pickup was parked at Pascal's cabin.

I rode up beside the house, tied my horse to a tree, and pounded on the door. Pascal and Flint were upset when I gave them the message. They told me to leave Thunder Hooves tied where she was and to get into Flint's truck. The three of us rode back to Grandmother's house.

When we got there, Flint parked the truck beside Cloud's. "You stay in the truck!" he ordered. He and Pascal ran for the house, leaving me alone.

"Please let her be all right," I whispered over and over to the wind. "Please don't blow her breath of life away. Please don't send the Spirit Horse for her—" I must have repeated that a hundred times as I waited for someone to come back outside.

Just when I was sure they had forgotten about me, the door opened, and Cloud stepped outside and closed it behind him.

The look on his face told me the worst had happened.

He walked up to the truck and leaned against the door with his back toward me.

"She's gone, Cry. Shima Sani is dead." He took a deep breath. "It was the fever. She just slipped away. There was nothing we could do. She was weak, but she talked to us. She was glad to have at least three of her sons with her at the last."

"I should have been in there," I said hoarsely.

"No, Cry. It was better for you to be out here."

"Did she say anything to me? Did she leave a message?" I desperately wanted her to leave something behind for me to hang on to.

"No. Nothing. She just talked a little." He must have sensed how I felt, and he added, "She probably would have said something for you, Cry, but she ran out of time."

He turned around and looked at me. He could see I was seconds from bursting into tears. I was trying to fight it, biting my lip and blinking my eyes, but it couldn't be held back. My grief just had to come out.

"I'm going to get the rest of the family." He headed for his truck and left.

I knew it would be all right if I went inside the house now, but it seemed too late. She was gone, and there didn't seem to be any point in going in.

49

I sat in the truck and waited. Gradually other cars and trucks began to arrive, and my other aunts and uncles and cousins made their way into the house. It was nearly dark before I could finally bring myself to leave the truck and go inside.

Shima Sani dead? No, it was impossible. She couldn't be dead. She was not ready to die. I had seen her only hours ago, and she had told me herself she was not ready to die!

I looked around the room at my seven uncles. They stood there, solemn and dry eyed. There would be no tears shed for Shima Sani, at least not in public. It would show weakness to weep.

My oldest uncle stepped forward and made the announcement.

"Hear me. Our mother is dead. Shima Sani is gone forever, and her name will not be spoken again." Then he quickly walked out of the house, and one by one the others followed him.

I sat there in numb silence and looked at the bundle of cedar branches on the floor. Later tonight they would be burned so the smoke could direct Shima Sani's spirit to the place it should go. *What place,* I wondered, *and where is it? Would the cedar smoke really help her find it?* I looked at the bundle of branches, which suddenly seemed small. I decided to go out and gather more. I wanted her to have enough smoke. I didn't want her spirit to get lost and wander in darkness.

For one year her name would not be spoken aloud by her

The bowl and the cup were old and fragile.

50

family. If she heard her name, she could not rest and would return. At the end of a year, cedar branches would be burned again in case her spirit had become lost the first time and needed a second chance. After that she would truly be gone forever, and her name could again be spoken.

Now it would begin. First, Grandmother's favorite bowl and cup would be taken to the burial ground. There, members of the family would use them to hollow out a place in the earth for her grave. The bowl and cup were old and fragile, and they were already chipped and cracked from many years of use. The grave diggers would have to be very careful as they scooped away a handful of dirt at a time with the bowl and cup. It took hours to dig a grave this way, but this is how it must be done. This is the way it was always done. A Kickapoo grave must never be dug with the white man's shovel or any of his metal tools. After the grave was dug, someone would stay behind to guard it. You couldn't leave an open grave unguarded; an evil spirit might jump into the hole and hide. Then it could carry away the spirit of the dead person after he was buried.

Two of my uncles had gone into the forest and searched until they found a hollow log large enough to place Grandmother's body inside. They trimmed it the right length and carried it home.

Grandmother's body was taken care of by my aunts. They dressed her in her best clothing, and her white hair was plaited into two neat braids. Her turquoise and silver rings were placed on her fingers, and a pair of new moccasins were placed on her feet. Beads had been sewn on the soles of the moccasins to show that these feet would never again walk in the earth but would walk only in a land beyond here. A new, red blanket was folded and draped over her left arm, and a few of her favorite things were placed in her right hand: some beaver teeth; a tiny obsidian arrowhead; and a piece of beadwork she had been working on when she died, along with enough beads to finish it after she reached the end of her journey.

When my aunts were finished, my uncles gently lifted Grandmother and laid her in the hollow log. All seven of them stood shoulder to shoulder and carried her to the burial ground. She was placed in the grave, and her bowl and cup were smashed against the log so they could never be used again. Everyone pushed the dirt over her with their hands, and leaves and twigs were scattered over the surface until there was no sign of a grave being there.

A terrible feeling of loneliness swept over me. It wasn't fair! Grandmother and I had been on a journey together. We had been searching for an answer, and now she was gone before our journey was finished. She had gone on alone without the answer. She had died being afraid of death.

"Oh, Grandmother, where are you now?" I cried.

As I walked up the path to the house, I saw a mourning stick outside the door. It was a stick driven into the ground, and it had black crow feathers attached to it to tell others there had been a death in this house.

My aunts placed grandmother's personal belongings on the pile of cedar branches. A fire was started, and we all stood there in the darkness and watched the flames destroy the last of Grandmother's life here on earth. Her possessions would be sent to her

Her bowl and cup were smashed against a log.

on the smoke that was rising up to the stars. The fire snapped and crackled until it had destroyed everything and only a few dying embers remained.

After the rest of the family had gone to their homes, I stood alone and watched as the last hot coal flickered and died.

"I'm sorry, Grandmother," I whispered. "I'm sorry I took too long to find the answer for you."

She had been right. Spring had not come for her this year.

It seemed impossible that she was gone. As I entered the cold, dark house, I lighted a lamp and sat down on the edge of the bed and looked around. Every trace of her had vanished. It was almost as if she had never existed. The only clothes hanging on the wall were mine. The quilts she had made were gone. All of her personal possessions were gone.

It was so quiet I could almost hear the snow falling outside. The room seemed dark and full of shadows. I turned up the lamp wick. The flame grew higher, but the room still seemed dark. I walked over to the stove and started a fire. My hands were red and stiff, and I was shaking from the cold. There was ice on the top of the water bucket, and it was over an hour before the fire warmed the house enough to melt the ice.

The wind had come up. He seemed louder than I had ever heard him. He was angry, and I could hear him beating against the house. I put more wood on the fire, but I couldn't get warm. I wondered if I would ever feel warm again without Grandmother here.

I crawled into bed with my clothes on, because it was too cold to take them off. I pulled the covers tightly around me, and still I shivered.

"Oh, Grandmother! I miss you!" I cried out. "The wind is so loud, the cold has never been colder, and the dark has never been darker. Are you somewhere safe and warm, or are you out

53

there in the frozen night, with the wind blowing your spirit away?"

I stuck my fingers in my ears and tried not to hear the wind. I would not speak to him. I was angry at him for letting Grandmother die. I wanted to fight back, but who can fight the wind? He whistled and blew the snow deeper around the house and taunted me. I lay in the darkness, alone and shivering in the empty bed.

As soon as I woke, I turned over to see if I had had a terrible dream and maybe Grandmother would be sleeping beside me, but she wasn't there. It was no dream; she was really gone.

I spent the morning sitting beside the window and watching the snow, but by noon I knew I had to find something to do. I dragged out the box of beads and set up the loom. It made me feel better to be busy. I worked quickly. Soon I had a piece long enough for a woman's belt. I decided to make some rosettes next. They always sold well, and I would need some money to live on. I didn't know if Flint or Cloud would help me, but even if they did, I didn't want to have to beg them for every penny to buy food. I would need a little money of my own.

I spent all day on beadwork. My neck and back were stiff, and my fingers were starting to drop some of the tiny beads. The sun was going down, and the house was getting dark. I lighted the lamp and pulled it closer to my work. As tired as I was, I didn't want to stop. It seemed important to keep doing something. Then I wouldn't think about how empty and lonely the house was.

It was late now, and I was making mistakes. I had to go back and restring some of my work. I would have to quit. I just hoped I was tired enough to go right to sleep and not lie in bed for hours, staring into the darkness.

At least I had gotten through the first day alone. I felt proud

54

of myself for doing so much work. Tomorrow I would do this much again, or maybe more. I would keep busy. Before I went to bed each night I would make lots of plans for the next day. I would have something to look forward to, and things wouldn't seem so bad.

I finished the last row of beads on the large rosette necklace I was making. This necklace had turned out better than any I had ever made. I would get a good price for it at the trading post. If the trader bought everything I had made, I would have forty dollars. That was more money than I had ever had in my life.

I looked at the necklace one last time before putting it into the box with the other beadwork. My eyes were tired from working so long by the flickering light of the kerosene lamp. I blew out the flame and got ready for bed. As I walked past the window, I looked outside at the sparkling snow.

The moon was full and beautiful and reflected on the snow so brightly I could see clearly as far as the barn. Thunder Hooves and War Cloud were both drinking from the water trough, when a sudden gust of wind sent snow flying off the roof of the barn and across their backs. I laughed as both horses broke away and ran a short distance and then turned to see what had frightened them. Thunder Hooves was beautiful in the moonlight. Her neck was arched and her tail was held high and, even though I was too far away to see, I knew her eyes would be wide and wild looking and her nostrils would be flared as she snorted in disgust that something had dared to bother her. So beautiful and so proud. I was lucky to have her. She was the one thing in this world I could love and call my own. I watched her a while longer as she pranced and pawed at the snow. War Cloud had gone back to the business of getting a drink, but Thunder Hooves still shied away from the area around the barn. The wind blew again, and she shook her head and trotted in a large circle. Maybe she smelled the scent of coyotes on the wind tonight. Maybe that was why she was nervous.

I was too tired to watch her any longer, so I threw another log into the stove and climbed into bed.

Tomorrow I would go riding. Thunder Hooves and I would run faster than the wind. With that picture in my mind, I fell asleep.

Chapter Five

I woke up early the next morning and my first thought was, *This is my second day alone without Grandmother. Today will be easier than yesterday, tomorrow will be better than today.* I was looking forward to my ride.

Thunder Hooves would be good company today. She would make me feel better. Maybe we could ride up as far as Bitter Water Creek. I could pack a lunch and spend most of the day riding. I glanced out the window. The clouds were low and heavy with snow. A blizzard seemed to be coming. *I had better not try to go as far as Bitter Water today. If we are caught in a blizzard, it will be dangerous.* We could at least go up to the ridge and back; that wouldn't take long. I wouldn't need to take a lunch for such a short ride. I pulled on my leather jacket and tied a scarf around my hair and walked outside.

The bright glare of the snow blinded me for a few seconds. The air was so cold I lost my breath. I stood on the porch and looked toward the barn. I couldn't see any of the horses in the corral. I hoped they were inside the barn, because I didn't want to walk all over the pasture looking for them. The snow was too deep.

I stepped into the snow and felt it go over the tops of my moccasins. It was so cold, the snow crunched underfoot as I made my way toward the barn.

It wasn't until I climbed through the fence that I saw it. Red ice. A river of red ice around the water trough.

"What in the world is that?" I asked aloud. I stooped over

and touched it with my fingers. "What would make the ice red?" Then I felt weak. Blood. Blood would make the ice red!

I stood up and walked around the corner of the barn, following the red river of frozen blood.

I wanted to scream when I saw it, but no sound came from my open mouth.

Thunder Hooves lay on her side, with three of her feet tangled in barbed wire. Blood was everywhere. The snow was red where she lay in a pool of blood.

I turned and ran, staggering and falling and running again. I ran until my lungs felt as if they would explode inside my chest. With every step I begged, "Let her be all right! Let Cloud save her!"

I couldn't get through the snow drifts fast enough. They seemed to pull at me, sucking at me to slow me down. Time after time I fell flat, sprawling in the crusty snow; time after time I struggled back to my feet and ran again. I couldn't see anything except Thunder Hooves lying there, tangled in the wire, helpless and hurting.

At last I staggered up to Cloud's house and beat on the door.

"Cloud!" I screamed, and before I could hit the door with my fists again it opened, and there stood my uncle.

"Thunder Hooves is hurt!" I panted. "She's tangled in wire, she's bleeding. Help—help her!"

He grabbed his coat off a peg behind the door.

"Let's go!" he said and started to run back to the barn.

I ran after him as fast as I could, but I was exhausted and soon fell far behind him.

"He can save her! He can save her!" I gasped with each breath. I had seen him save many injured animals. He had a gift for healing animals. He would save her!

Soon he was out of sight, and I knew he had probably already

All the life had been drained out of me.

59

reached Thunder Hooves. My legs were shaking, and my throat was raw from sucking in the frosty air.

The barn came into sight. Cloud had seen me coming and was heading toward me.

He met me at the bottom of the hill.

"It's too late. She's dead," he said.

I shook my head. "No—I—ran—fast—you can—save her!" I gasped.

He shook his head again. "She's been dead for hours. She died last night. She was already dead when you saw her. It looks like she was running and hit some ice and slid into the wire— well, she bled to death."

I shook my head again. "No—" My lips formed other words, but there was no sound.

"I'm sorry, Cry. If it helps any, she probably didn't feel any pain. It was so cold last night. She lost so much blood so fast— it couldn't have taken long."

I could hear myself screaming and cursing and screaming some more. I threw myself down in the snow and beat at it with my fists.

Grandmother and Thunder Hooves both gone in two days! No! No! It couldn't be happening! I had lost everything! Everything!

Cloud didn't speak. He just stood nearby while my grief and anger ran their course. I thought I would never stop crying, but finally I did. I just sat in the snow, numb and empty and sick.

Cloud reached down and picked me up in his arms as if I were a small child and carried me the long distance back to his house.

I rested in his arms like a limp rag. I couldn't move one muscle in my body. All the life had drained out of me, just as it had drained out of Thunder Hooves.

Chapter Six

The blizzard came that night. The wind howled, and the snow piled up fast and deep. All I could think of was the fresh, white snow burying Thunder Hooves, covering her up in a white blanket of death, hiding the red ice, hiding her river of frozen blood.

The storm blew all night and all the next day and into the next night. I slept most of the time, drifting in and out of wakefulness and sleep. I didn't want to remember the ache inside of me. I didn't want to think about life being one loss after another, always losing something, never gaining anything. My mind mercifully blocked out everything around me and let me sleep. I remembered Cloud waking me up a couple of times and feeding me, but I don't remember what I ate or if we talked. I only remembered the storm raging outside as if it would last forever.

Somehow the next few days passed, and my heart hurt a little less than it had.

I didn't say it out loud, but in my heart I felt that the wind had killed Thunder Hooves. It was the wind that had frightened her into running. The wind had been angry at me and had punished me by killing the last thing I had in the world. That's what I thought, but I was too afraid to say it, for the wind might kill me next.

I began to wonder how we had gotten all the Indian gods in the first place.

"Cloud, where did our religion come from?"

He looked surprised. "What do you mean?"

"Who started doing the ceremonies? How did they know

what to do or when to do it? Who made up the songs and dances? How did it all get started?"

He shrugged. "How should I know? It is all old. The old, ancient ones started it a long time ago, I guess."

"How long ago?"

"How do I know?"

"A thousand years ago?" I asked.

"Maybe."

"What did the Indians do before that?"

"Who knows?"

"That's just it! Nobody knows anything about the Indians! Anthropologists say we came from Asia across the Bering Straits and started out as yellow-skinned people and somehow turned red halfway here."

Cloud laughed and joined in, "And others say we came from the South Seas and we had brown skin and turned red later. Funny how the experts think we can change the color of our skin." He laughed again.

"Where do you think we really came from?" I was serious again.

"I think the Indian people were created here." He waved his arm around him, meaning here in America. "I don't think we came from any other place or any other people. We have always been here, we are The People, The Land."

"Maybe that is true," I agreed, "but if there is only one Indian people, why are there so many Indian religions? Even in our own family, we don't use the true Kickapoo religion. We mix Navajo with Kickapoo because Grandmother and Grandfather never could agree on which was right. Is the Kickapoo religion better, or is the Navajo better, or the Sioux? Who is right? How can they all be right when they are all so different?" I pleaded for an answer.

"You make me tired with all your questions. I don't know the answers. Stop thinking about it. What difference does it make, anyway?" He had had enough.

"Yes, I guess you're right. What difference does it make, anyway?" I repeated, but I had an uneasy feeling inside that what you believe made a very big difference, or it wouldn't bother me so much.

I had been staying with my uncle for two weeks. One morning he came in and sat down beside me.

"Cry, do you feel like talking?"

"What about?" I asked. I hoped he was not going to mention Grandmother or Thunder Hooves, because today was the first day I hadn't cried. I was afraid if he mentioned either of them I would start crying again.

"You know, you can't go back and live in that house alone. For one thing, you're too young, and for another thing—well, it's not a good idea," he said and started pulling off his coat.

I nodded. He was going to ask me to stay here with him! I was excited. I could cook and keep house for Cloud, and he could bring home food for us. It would be perfect. We wouldn't have to be alone. Before I could tell him how happy I was, he continued.

"Anyway, I've been thinking. You can't stay there by yourself, and you can't stay here with me because I'll be leaving soon—"

"Leaving?" I asked weakly.

"Yeah. Look, Cry, there's nothing here for either of us anymore. There never was very much, but now there is nothing. I can do a little hunting and a little trapping and barely support myself, but game is getting scarce, and the price of pelts has gone down again. I can't support both of us."

"I can sell beadwork!" I said eagerly.

He laughed. "Oh, Cry! You are thinking about a handful of dollars. I'm sick of being half-hungry all the time." He stood up

"You can't stay here yourself, and I'll be leaving."

and paced the floor. "Do you know that Indians live in the worst poverty of any people in America? This is our land. We were here first, and now we are living in worse conditions than any other people here. I'm sick of it, and I'm getting out. I've been thinking about leaving a long time. I think the signs are right to go now. You'll go too. There is nothing to hold us here."

"Then you are taking me with you?" I asked, afraid of the answer.

"No, because I don't know where I'm going or what I'll do. Flint is living in town now. I guess he is doing all right. That would be the best place for you, too. I'll sell everything we own

64

and split the money with you. Then I'll take you into town and get you a place to live. You'll have to get a job, but until you do, Flint can keep an eye on you."

"I can't! I've never lived in town. I don't know how to do anything. How can I get a job? What will I do?"

"You'll manage," he answered simply. "You'll learn how to survive, and Flint can help you out."

"No! I want to stay here!" I said stubbornly.

"You can't. You would starve to death, or else you would be fair game for any drunken Indians who knew you were up here alone." He looked at me meaningfully, and I got the message.

"How soon do I have to leave?"

"I'll ask the trader to come out tomorrow. I'll sell him everything I can. We should be out of here in a couple of days."

"Where will you go?"

"I don't know," he said.

"You must have some plans," I insisted.

"No. All I know is that I want to get as far away from here as I can. I want a fresh start, and I want to have some of the things that other people have!" he said with determination. "This is best for you, too. Cry. You'll see. There will be something for you in the city. You'll meet people. You'll learn a new way of life. Maybe you'll find someone to marry. Whatever happens to you, it's got to be better than living like this." He picked up his tin cup and hurled it across the room. It hit the wall and clattered to the floor.

I looked at the empty cup for a moment and then asked, "Will you keep in touch with me?"

"Sure, you know I will. As soon as I find out who I am and where I'm going, I'll write to you. Maybe I'll send for you," he said.

I didn't believe him. As soon as he was gone he would be every bit as lost to me as Grandmother and Thunder Hooves.

65

I would never see him again. I kept my eyes on the empty tin cup he had just thrown away. How very much I felt like that empty cup!

Cloud put his coat back on and went after the rest of my things and brought them back to his place. He began sorting out all he owned, putting things to keep into one pile and things to sell to the trader into another pile. He was keeping very little. All my beadwork was put out for the trader to buy. I had planned to sell it to the trader anyway, but now I wanted to keep it with me a little longer. I didn't want to part with everything so soon. I picked out one bead necklace and put it on for awhile, but when I saw Cloud looking at me, I took it off and put it back on the pile for the trader.

After the trader had left, taking everything with him, I felt that I had lost everything in the world. Cloud stood on the porch beside me as we watched the trader drive off with everything we had owned bouncing around in the back of his truck.

"We'll leave tomorrow morning," he said. "We'll go to town and find Flint first. He might know of a place where you can stay. I'll give you sixty dollars, and that will get you started. After that, you are on your own."

I hardly slept all night. There had been too many changes too fast, and now I would be leaving here forever. This was the only place I had ever known, and I had never been more than a few miles from here. Now I felt as if I was being sent to another world, outside and far away.

As soon as it was dawn, Cloud loaded things into the back of his rusty old pickup truck. Sleepy-eyed, I followed him down the path from the house for the last time.

Someday I'll come back here, I thought. *This is where I belong. This is my home.*

Cloud reached over and handed me a piece of jerky. "Here's

breakfast. I hope you never have to eat such poor food again," he said. He started the truck. The motor was cold and growled over and over before it would start. I hoped it wouldn't start at all, and we could stay here at least for a few more days, but it did start. Soon we were on our way on the rough road that led to the highway that would take us to town.

Soon we were on our way on the rough road that led to the highway that would take us to town.

We were almost to town before I realized I still hadn't eaten the jerky. It had been lying in my cold hands so long I had forgotten it. I bit off a piece and chewed it. It was as hard and dry as a piece of old leather. I might as well have been chewing on my moccasin for all the flavor it had.

It didn't take Cloud long to find Flint. He was working in a lumber yard. I waited in the car while the two of them stood a distance away and talked. Occasionally one of them would look toward the truck, and I guessed that Flint was not very happy about having me dumped on him. Finally both of them walked back to the truck.

I rolled down the window, and Flint bent his tall frame almost double to speak to me.

"I guess you'll be staying here," he said. "I know of a place down the road where you can get a cheap room. Cloud will take you there. I'll stop in and see you after work tonight."

I nodded in agreement. I had no choice, and we all knew it.

In a few more minutes Cloud pulled up in front of a place with several rows of small cabins. The sign in front read, "Pine Valley Court."

Cloud got out of the truck and walked into the office. In a minute he came back with a man and motioned for me to come along.

I hurried after them as they walked to a small cabin at the end of the row.

The man unlocked the door and pushed it open, motioning for us to go in first.

I stood in the center of the living room and looked around. It was about the size of the house Grandmother and I had had, but this was so nice. There was a rug on the floor and curtains on the windows. There was a small kitchen off to one side, with a gas stove and a real refrigerator. I could have hot or cold food any time I wanted! There was a bathroom with a real bathtub, where I could stretch out in hot water instead of bathing out of an old tin washbasin as I had back home. The furniture was finer than any I had ever seen, and there was a big bed off by itself in another room.

"I'm sorry it's so small, but for one person it would be all right." The manager apologized for the size, not knowing that it was the best place I had ever been in.

"It's completely furnished," he said. "Linens, dishes, everything. It's fifty dollars a month or twenty dollars a week."

"We'll take it," Cloud said.

"When do you want to move in?" the manager asked.

"She already has," Cloud replied. He paid the manager for two weeks' rent and handed me twenty dollars to live on. He left me there and went for my suitcase.

The manager gave me the key and left just as Cloud came back through the door with my suitcase. He set it down beside me and looked around.

"You'll be all right," he said. "Flint will come over later. If you need anything, tell him. Oh, one more thing. It might be a good idea to tell people you are eighteen years old instead of fourteen."

"I'm fifteen now," I said. "I had a birthday."

"Oh." He looked embarrassed. "I guess I forgot."

"Everyone did," I said.

Cloud couldn't wait to leave. I wanted to keep him with me just a little longer, but I couldn't think of any way to hold on to him.

"You're settled now," he said. "I guess I'll be going." He walked back outside and I followed him.

"Cloud—" I wanted to beg him to stay, but I knew he wouldn't, so I just said, "Be careful." That wasn't what I had wanted to say, but I couldn't find the right words to tell him how I felt. I wished I could reach out and touch him, hold him for one second; but that would be a sign of weakness, and he would hate it. So I folded my arms in front of me so I wouldn't be tempted to touch him.

"Good-bye, Cry," he said and climbed into his old truck. He gave me a quick smile and then drove away. I knew I would never see him again.

I watched until his truck was out of sight. When he had gone, I retreated to my cabin and closed the door behind me and locked it. I opened my suitcase and put my clothes in a drawer and hung

69

my dress in the closet. In less than three minutes I was unpacked and moved in. I walked around and around the rooms, examining each and every little thing, turning the stove on and off, and opening the refrigerator time after time.

It was a good place, better than I had ever had before. I knew I would be here at least two weeks; the rent was paid for that long. I had twenty dollars, but I didn't know how much food twenty dollars would buy. I had never shopped for food anywhere except at the trading post. I had done that only a few times, so I wasn't sure how much things cost, but it couldn't be very much.

I spent the rest of the afternoon walking back and forth and peeking out the window, hoping Flint would come.

About the middle of the afternoon, I heard tires grinding across the gravel driveway. I leaped to my feet and hurried to the window to look outside.

It was Flint! I tugged the door open and went outside to meet him.

He got out of his pickup, walked up to the cabin, and stuck his head through the door.

"Everything OK?" he asked.

"Yes. Cloud is gone," I said. I hoped he might say something about where Cloud was going.

"Didn't think he'd stick around." He leaned up against the door. "Guess you need some food. Get in the truck, and I'll drive you to a store."

I grabbed my twenty-dollar bill and my key and climbed into the truck beside Flint.

There was a store only a few blocks away. It seemed huge. It was ten times bigger than the trading post and full of bright lights and rows and rows of shelves of food.

Flint pulled out a wire cart and started pushing it down the aisles. At first I was so overwhelmed by so much food that I went down two rows without putting anything in the basket. We had to go back and start over. Then I started picking up everything that looked good and putting it into the basket.

"Hold on a minute. You don't have enough money for all that stuff," Flint said. He put a lot of it back on the shelves. "Just get what you need. After you get a job, you can buy what you want." He put a can of lard and a small bag of flour into the cart. "You can live cheap on fry bread and eggs."

I could see I was going to end up eating the same thing here that I had eaten back on the reservation. Things weren't going to be better, after all. I let Flint pick out the rest of the food, but my eyes were still on the bright cans and packages of wonderful things like peaches and chocolate candy and roast beef. The groceries in the cart cost seventeen dollars. Flint took my twenty-dollar bill and handed me the change. I couldn't believe everything cost so much. No wonder he hadn't let me buy all I wanted. It would probably have cost a hundred dollars.

He drove me back to the cabin and sat in a chair while he waited for me to put my food away. He was looking at a newspaper and marking in it with a pencil. After I had put the food away, he motioned for me to come and sit beside him.

"I marked some jobs for you to check tomorrow. You might have to try many places before anyone will hire you. Some people won't hire you because you're an Indian, and some won't want you because you've never worked before. You'll just have to keep trying until you get a job somewhere. You had better tell them you're eighteen years old."

"Cloud told me that, too," I said.

"Yeah. Well, we talked about it and figured if people knew you were only fourteen, it might cause trouble. Another thing—don't talk to any strange men, and don't invite anyone back to your apartment with you."

"Why?"

"Things are different here. You have to be careful. I'll keep an eye on you as much as I can, but I can't be around all the time. If you need help, you know where I work." He handed the newspaper to me and stood up. "I'll go now."

"Can't you stay a little while?" I asked.

He shook his head. "No, I have some things to do. You'll be all right. I'll check back in a few days," he said as he opened the door. "Keep your door locked all the time," he cautioned as he pulled it shut behind him.

I checked the door to make sure it was locked. "Everybody keeps saying that I'll be all right. I don't think they believe that any more than I do," I muttered to myself as I went into my little kitchen to fix some dinner.

When I climbed out of bed the next morning, I was filled with dread. I had to start looking for a job right away, and I didn't know where to go or what to do after I got there. I put on the only good outfit I owned, pulled on my moccasins, brushed my hair, and picked up the newspaper Flint had left.

I walked sixteen blocks to reach the first place listed in the paper. I had hardly walked through the door before I was told the job was already taken. It was three more blocks to the second store that had an opening. I did a little better. At least I was allowed to fill out an application. It didn't take long; all I could put on it was my name, address and age. My age was a lie. When there is no education and no experience to write down, the page looks pretty blank.

The rest of the morning was spent the same way, walking from store to store, filling out applications, and watching people's eyebrows go up when they read my name, Crying Wind.

At the next place I applied, the personnel manager gave me a cold look over the top of her glasses and asked, "Who sent you here? Was it the Equal Employment or Civil Liberties or who?"

72

I shook my head. I didn't have the slightest idea what she was talking about.

She dropped my application on her desk as if it were something dirty, put her hands on her hips, and said, "Well, you can go right back to whoever sent you here, and tell them we've already filled our minority quota. We don't want any more of you—you people!"

By "you people" I figured she meant Indians and that there was something wrong with being an Indian.

The eleventh store I stopped at was a large department store. There was an opening for a salesclerk in the kitchenware department. The man who spoke to me seemed to think I would be able to sell pots and pans and can openers, so he said I could have the job starting the next day. I would be paid thirty-five dollars a week.

I jumped at the chance. I didn't think I could face filling out any more applications. I was exhausted from walking all over town. I was grateful for any kind of a job. I knew that Flint would be relieved that I found work and could support myself.

It was twenty-five blocks from the apartment to the store, but I was so proud that I had a job, I didn't notice.

On the first day of my new job, I felt numb. I was sure I would do something wrong and be fired. I almost didn't show up, but I knew I would have to have money, so I gritted my teeth and went. Somehow I got through the morning. Finally my boss said I could go to lunch.

"Where do I go?" I asked.

"It's upstairs." He gave a nod of his head without looking at me. I saw a flight of stairs tucked away in a corner of the room. When I got to the top of the stairs, there were two doors. On one door there was a red sign that said, "Keep Out," so I carefully opened the other door. It opened into a huge dark room with boxes stacked all over. It was dusty and cluttered. Surely this couldn't be the lunchroom. There must be a door on the other side of the room. I worked my way between the rows of boxes and came to the opposite corner. Instead of a door, there was a pile of old, broken mannequins. Arms and legs and heads were stacked in a heap, with more heads lined up against the wall. I knew they were made of plaster, but I felt as if their painted eyes were looking at me. I backed up. I wanted out of there. I almost expected some force to pull the mannequin parts together to form a multi-legged monster that would chase me. I hurried back across the room without looking behind me. I was being silly; I knew that. After all, I was fifteen. Wasn't that old enough to be on your own in the world? Why was I so afraid of everything?

I heard voices coming from the door marked "Keep Out." I opened the door a crack and saw about a dozen women eating their lunches around a long table. I walked inside the room and tried to smile, but my face felt stiff. A couple of them looked up and nodded, but the others ignored me and went on eating and talking. I picked a seat on the corner and put my wrinkled, brown sack on the table. I looked around and saw that everyone else had neat, little lunch boxes with flowers and bright colors. I took my sack off the table and held it in my lap.

I had a sandwich of two pieces of fry bread and a fried egg. I felt starved. When I bit into my sandwich, I discovered that I hadn't cooked my egg long enough. The yolk was cold and runny and dripped into my lap. I was so afraid that everyone was watching me, I wouldn't look up. I took a few bites, but the half-raw egg just would not slide down my throat. I gave up, wrapped my sandwich in my wrinkled brown sack, threw it all in the trash, and left.

I felt foolish. I wondered if any of them knew I had gone in the wrong door and had wandered around lost in a storage room. Me lost! I had walked miles and miles in the deepest forest and across dusty plains, and I had never forgotten a rock or a stick or a tree. I had never been lost. Now, here in a simple building, I had become confused and got lost. In the forest back home I could have found a blue-jay feather on a mountainside a mile away. Here in the city I couldn't find a lunchroom up one flight of stairs.

My clothing was the same as anyone else's—perhaps a little old-fashioned, but not so much that I looked odd. I wore gathered, cotton skirts, just a little longer than the other girls' skirts, with long-sleeved, cotton blouses. I was proud of my moccasins. I had made them from an elk my uncles had killed. I had carefully sewn them together and used leather thongs and a silver concho to fasten them. They were soft and comfortable. I could walk miles in them, and my feet would not grow tired. The moccasins were silent on the city pavement. It was comforting to look at them on my feet and pretend I was still at home, stepping carefully through the forest. Yes, my clothes were a little different, but I didn't mind looking a little different.

There was a girl at work named Betty, who was beautiful. Her clothes were expensive and fit perfectly. Whenever she was around, I began to notice that my blouses were too loose and my skirts too long. Her hair curled around her face. I was determined to look like she did, but no matter what I did to my hair at night, it would end up hanging straight down my back in the morning. After several sleepless nights of trying to rest with curlers and pins in my hair, I gave up and let my hair go its own way.

Betty wore very high heels, which click-clicked as she walked around the store. My elk-hide mocassins sh-shhhed. Suddenly the moccasins I had taken so much pride in looked out of place, and I began to feel foolish. One day a customer looked at my feet and laughed, and I was angry and embarrassed. During my

75

lunch hour I hurried out and bought a pair of shiny black shoes with heels as high as the other girls'. From then on I click-clicked as I walked around the store, and no one laughed at my shoes anymore. At night, when I came home from spending eight hours on my feet in those high heels, I would kick them off as soon as I came through the door and put on my old, friendly moccasins.

One day a Cherokee Indian boy about my age came into the store. I was happy to see someone like me. We talked a few minutes, but by his words and actions it was clear he was what the Indians call an "apple," someone who is red on the outside but white on the inside—an Indian who wants to be a white person. Sometimes I felt that I was the opposite, white on the outside and red on the inside. I wondered if there was any fruit like that, that I could be called.

Betty was nice to me and even gave me some of her clothes that she was tired of, but I never looked as good in them as she did. There is just no way you can make a hundred pounds of skin and bones look like anything except a hundred pounds of skin and bones.

Days ran into nights and the nights ran into days, and weeks crept by.

I lay on my bed and stared at the ceiling. I could hear the faucet dripping in the bathroom, but it seemed like too much effort to get up and turn it off. I would do it later. I turned over on my side. I saw the telephone shoved under the edge of the chair. I had lived here six months and never used it. I had never called anyone or received a call from anyone.

I got off the bed, knelt on the floor, and pulled the telephone out from under the chair. It was dusty, and I wiped it off. The telephone had come with the room, as had the rest of the utilities. I hadn't even thought about it. It was just something that was always in the way when I wanted to put a book or a glass of

76

water on the night table, so I had stuck it under the chair and forgotten about it.

Now I wished I had someone to call. Betty! I could call Betty! I pulled the phone book out of the drawer and looked up Woodard. There were a lot of people named Woodard, but no Betty Woodard was listed.

I let the phone book fall shut, and then I opened it again— there must be someone in town I could call. Flint didn't have a phone, but there must be someone to talk to. I found the number for the time and temperature and dialed it carefully. I had used a telephone only a couple of times in my entire life.

"Hello?" I said when I heard a click at the other end, "Can you tell me—" It was a few seconds before I realized there was just a recorded message at the other end of the line. I listened to it three times, "Time 7:30 PM—temperature 72 degrees—Have a good evening and when you are looking for a bank you can trust be sure and—"

I began looking through the yellow pages, starting with *A* and going from one advertisement to the next until I reached the *C's*, where the churches were listed. I had not realized the town had so many churches. My finger trailed down the page and rested on "Trinity Evangelical United Brethren Church, Rev. Glenn O. McPherson, Pastor." I read on down the page, but my eyes rested again on the church with the long name. Somehow that name seemed to stand out more than any of the others. I turned the page and looked at more advertisements, but in a few minutes I turned back to the church listings and hunted again for the church with the long name.

Maybe I will call that church, I thought. *I could call that man named McPherson and ask him something. Then I would have someone to talk to, not a recording. I can always hang up whenever I want. I can even give him some other name. I could*

77

ask him a question about something, maybe about his church. I began dialing. One ring—two rings—

"Hello, this is Reverend McPherson speaking."

My mouth felt dry. Now what? Maybe I should just hang up.

"May I help you?" came the soft voice on the phone.

"I—I—I was just, ah, wondering about—about your church— I wondered what it was like—I mean—what you did there?" I sounded foolish. I shouldn't have done this. Whatever had possessed me to do such a dumb thing?

"We worship God the best way we know how." He paused. "If you could tell me exactly what you want to know I could be more helpful—"

"I don't know what to ask—" I blurted out. "I'm new here. I just saw your name in the phone book and—" I could feel my face burning. Why didn't I just hang up?

"You would be welcome to visit our church anytime." He sounded friendly.

"No, I don't think I want to do that. I don't know anyone— never mind. I'm sorry I bothered you."

"Wait—don't hang up. I could give you some booklets that explain what our church is all about. You can read them and decide if you would like to attend our church or not. I could mail them to you."

That sounded like a good idea. I could get some mail, and I could get off this telephone. "All right. My name is Crying Wind—" and I gave him my address.

"Oh, you only live four blocks from the church. You are just right up the street from us."

My heart sank. That was why the name of the church had stuck in my mind tonight, why it had seemed familiar. I passed that little brick church on my way to and from work. This was awful! I had called someone right in the neighborhood!

"I'm making a house call near you. If you aren't busy, I'll

drop off these books on my way. You can have them tonight," he said.

"OK," I answered weakly. I should have told him I wasn't going to be home, but I hadn't thought fast enough.

I hung up the telephone and slid it back under the chair. That was were it could stay! My one and only phone call I had made since moving here, and it had gotten me into a big mess! Now what was I going to do? I hurried to my closet and got out my coat. I would leave and just not be there when he came. Then I stopped. He would probably come back another time, and I would have to go through this again. It was better to get it over with. I hung my coat back in the closet.

I didn't have to wait long until I heard footsteps outside and someone knocking on the door of the cabin next to mine. I held my breath. No one lived on either side of me, so I knew it had to be Reverend McPherson searching for me. He knocked on my door, and I jumped.

The door seemed to weigh a ton as I slowly pulled it open. A small man wearing glasses and dressed in a gray suit stood before me.

"I'm Reverend McPherson."

I nodded. "Come in."

Another mistake. I shouldn't have invited him inside.

I sat on the edge of the couch, and he took a chair opposite me.

"I won't take up much of your time. I'm sure you have something to do on such a nice evening." He smiled.

"No, I wasn't doing anything." *Another mistake,* I thought, *I should have told him I was leaving soon, and he wouldn't stay long. I'm doing everything wrong.*

"I brought you everything I could think of that might help you." He put a handful of booklets on the table, "I will try to answer any questions—that is, if you have any."

I twisted my fingers together and stared at him. He looked

embarrassed, but I had the feeling it wasn't for himself. He was embarrassed for me. Somehow he knew how awkward I felt.

"How old are you?"

"Eighteen."

"You don't look eighteen. You aren't married, are you?"

"No."

"Good. Well, I just meant that eighteen is very young." He tried to look around the room without being obvious. "Do you have a relative or a girlfriend who lives here with you?"

"No."

"You aren't from around here, are you?" He already knew the answer.

"No. I just moved here a few months ago." I knew I wasn't saying enough, so I added, "I work at Hawkins Department Store."

"Oh, my wife goes there sometimes. Do you like your job?"

"It's all right, I guess."

He turned his hat over in his hands a few times, and silence hung heavy in the room.

"Who is your God?" I asked in a strange, tight voice that seemed far away and not my own at all. I couldn't believe I had asked that question. Surely it hadn't come from me!

He smiled. "That is a big question. I could give you a lot of pat answers or tell you what the great theologians say, but I don't think that's what you want to hear. To me, God is the Creator of everything. He made man, but man fell into sin. God loved man so much that He made a blood sacrifice of His only Son so man could be washed clean from sin and have everlasting life. I believe much more than that, but that is it in a nutshell—I'm sure you've heard that many times before."

I shook my head. "No, I haven't heard that before."

"Have you ever read the Bible?"

"I don't have one. I've never read it. Bibles are for church people."

"Bibles are for everyone. I'll give you one. I don't have one with me tonight, but I'll either bring one or mail one to you. What church have you attended in the past?"

"None." I swallowed hard. "I've never been to a church."

He couldn't hide the look of surprise on his face. "I see." He was silent for a moment then asked quietly, "I don't want to embarrass you or to pry, but would you like to tell me what you do believe, and then we could go from there?"

I took a deep breath and pointed to some of my drawings hanging on the wall behind him.

He turned and looked at the sketches of various Indian gods and the signs telling their legends.

"I'm—" I didn't want to say half-breed. "I'm part Indian. My grandmother taught me about the old religions. I believe in the old gods. I believe in the wind."

I clenched my teeth and waited for him to laugh, but he didn't. I felt some of the tension drain from me.

"I'm very ignorant about this subject," he said, "I thought Indians believed in a Great Spirit."

I told him a few things about the old religion.

"I've often wondered about some of the Indian customs. Some of them seem very strange to us." And then he added, "I suppose some of our customs seem strange to you."

"Yes. There is even a story about that. A white man went to a Kickapoo funeral, and he saw the Indians putting food in the grave, and the white man asked when would the dead Indian eat the food. A Kickapoo thought for a moment. Then he asked the white man, 'Don't you put flowers on the grave of your dead ones?' 'Yes,' replied the white man. 'Well, then,' said the Indian. 'When the dead white man smells the flowers, that is when the dead Indian will eat the food.'"

81

He laughed, but not at me, only at the story.

He didn't say much more, and he didn't stay long. He said he had to leave and visit some more people, but he invited me to come to his church, and then he left.

I told myself I was lucky to get off that easily. It was nice of him not to embarrass me or try to convert me. He was probably a pretty nice man. One thing for sure though—I had learned my lesson. I would never use that telephone again! That little machine could get a person into a lot of trouble!

Chapter Eleven

After Flint decided I wasn't going to be a pest, he started coming around more often. We were closer than we had ever been. Since I had no other family or friends in town, I looked forward to seeing him. I was always disappointed on the evenings he didn't come.

The next time he did show up, it was to bring sad news.

"Your Uncle Pascal is dead," he said simply.

"Dead?" I tried to think of the last time I'd seen him. It had been when Grandmother had died. "I didn't know there was anything wrong with him."

"There wasn't." Flint shuffled his feet a moment. Then the truth came out. Pascal had eaten dinner at a friend's house, he had played with the children before they went to bed, and he had sat and talked for about an hour. He hadn't said anything special, just talked about the past and how most of his friends were gone now and he was alone. Then about 10:00 PM, he left and walked home. They figured within an hour after he had arrived at his house, he committed suicide by shooting himself in the head with his shotgun. Flint was kind enough to spare me the details, but some very ugly pictures flashed through my mind.

"But why would he do that?" I asked.

"He was lonely." Flint slumped into a chair. "We're all lonely."

"Yeah," I said almost in a whisper. Even now, loneliness hung in the air like a fog. Flint and I were together, yet we were two of the loneliest people who had ever lived.

We sat there a long time listening to the storm outside. I was thinking about Uncle Pascal. I couldn't remember very much about him. I couldn't even clearly remember what he looked like, and now he was gone. I would never see him again. What was worse, I probably wouldn't even miss him. I looked across the room at Flint and was surprised to see how upset he was. He had lost a brother. They had been fairly close. They were both bachelors. Maybe Flint was thinking they had a lot in common and was wondering if he would end up like that.

Suddenly his eyes met mine and he gave me one of those funny, crooked smiles that didn't really mean anything.

"Know what I'm going to do, Cry?" He stood up.

"No, what?" I tried to sound casual.

"I'm going out and get drunk. I'm going to get drunker than I've ever been in my life and then—" He stopped.

"And then what?" I stood up and walked toward the door, more in an attempt to keep him in than to let him out.

"Nothing," he said.

He stepped around me, put his hand on the doorknob, and looked back at me.

"He was right."

"Who was right?" I dreaded the answer.

"Pascal was right." His voice cracked, and I knew I couldn't let him leave alone, or I would never see him alive again.

"I'm coming with you Flint," I said. I grabbed my coat. "I don't want to be alone." It was true. I didn't want to be alone, and I didn't want him to be alone either.

"Sure, why not? I'm not going far."

He drove to the nearest liquor store and left me sitting in the car while he went inside. He returned with several sacks, each containing a bottle of liquor.

Then he drove back to my apartment and handed me one of the bottles.

"Here kid," he said and shoved one of the sacks toward me.

84

"Don't leave yet, Flint. Please come inside." I picked up the bottles and opened the car door. "You can drink here as well as anyplace else, and it's nice and warm." I didn't want to leave him alone when he was this depressed.

Before he could say no, I hurried inside and took all the liquor with me. He didn't seem to have any will of his own left and followed me without an argument.

Flint opened the first bottle of whiskey, poured some into a glass, and handed it to me. He took the bottle with him and stretched out on the couch.

"Here's to a wasted warrior," he said and began pouring the liquor down his throat like he was trying to drown himself.

I had seen my uncles and my grandfather drink this way before. For many Indians, heavy drinking is a way of life. The stories about the "red man and firewater" weren't far from the truth. Unlike the white man who drinks to be sociable, the red man drinks to get drunk. He drinks to forget that he belongs no place; that he is a relic of the past. The two largest killers of Indians are alcoholism and suicide. In that room that night we had all the makings for both.

I took a sip from my glass and blinked my eyes as the liquor burned my throat. I had a feeling that really I shouldn't be drinking, but I pushed it to the back of my mind. Why shouldn't I drink? Why shouldn't I? What difference did it make? Who cared, anyway? By the time I had finished my drink, Flint had finished the bottle, and we were both feeling the false security that goes with alcohol. Our brains were numb. Flint would rattle on and on, and I would laugh at anything he said without knowing whether it was funny or not. Instead of passing time, the whiskey seemed to make it stand still, and instead of escaping the present, we were suspended in it.

My tongue felt thick, and my head ached. I was tired. "I'm going to bed now, Flint," I said sleepily.

"OK, kid, I'll leave." He picked up the last bottle and headed toward the door, but before he reached it, he crashed into a chair and fell, spread-eagle on the floor. We laughed until our sides ached.

"You'd better stay here tonight. You can sleep on the couch. I'll get some blankets for you." I weaved my way to the closet. By the time I got back, he had passed out. He was in the same position as when he had fallen. One hand still had a firm grip on the unopened bottle. I didn't try to wake him; I just spread a blanket over him and left him asleep on the floor.

I didn't wake up until late the next morning. I knew before I moved that I'd made a terrible mistake. My head ached, my eyes hurt, my stomach was in knots, and I wanted to die. I had a hangover. I lay in bed for nearly an hour before I could get up and face the day. I hoped I wouldn't be fired for not showing up at work. I would tell them I was sick. That was the truth; I couldn't have felt worse if I had had every disease known to mankind.

I walked unsteadily to where Flint was still asleep. It didn't look like he had moved all night, but then I saw that the bottle had been opened and was beside him, empty. Sometime during the night he had regained consciousness, finished drinking the last bottle of whiskey, and passed out again.

I left him alone. He would have to sleep it off. Besides, I didn't feel like talking to anyone now. I didn't think I could move my tongue.

I sat and held my head and drank coffee until noon, when Flint finally sat up and looked around.

"How do you feel, kid?" he asked and tenderly touched his head with his fingertips.

"Terrible."

"Yeah. But we had a good time, didn't we?" He gave me that crooked smile again.

I didn't answer. I hadn't had a good time. I was still lonely and afraid and so was he. On top of all that, we were both sick.

"I'll never drink again," I said and handed him a cup of coffee.

"Why not?" he asked and made a face as he swallowed some coffee.

"It's stupid. You drink all night, and when you wake up the next morning, nothing has changed."

"Well, it makes you forget," he said.

"I didn't forget anything."

He took another drink of coffee. "No," he said softly, "neither did I."

We sat there and stared at the empty bottles lying on the floor.

"What else is there?" he asked.

"I don't know, but there must be something." My head was starting to hurt again. "There must be something else to life, Flint. Otherwise—otherwise, what's the point to anything?"

"That's the joke. There is no point to anything." He laughed harshly. "Pascal found that out."

I felt tears coming to my eyes. "Flint, why doesn't anyone love us?"

He swallowed hard. "I don't know."

I wiped my eyes on my sleeves. "It looks like somebody, some-where would love us."

He reached across the table and tugged on my hair. "It's OK, kid. You and I will stick together and lick the world."

I laughed in spite of the way I felt. "Sure, Flint. You and I will stick together and lick the whole world."

He stayed about an hour longer. We talked about the weather and hunting season and a dozen other subjects that didn't mean anything, but we kept our minds busy so we wouldn't think too much. By the time he left, I was feeling better, and he was too. He would get through today all right, and maybe this week, but one of these nights he would start thinking about Pascal again. Maybe he would have too much to drink and maybe—maybe no one would be around to stop him from killing himself.

What happens when you die? I kept asking myself. I thought I had run away from that question when I left the valley, but it had reached out and touched me again. Grandmother hadn't known; Uncle Pascal hadn't known. Did anyone know? You couldn't know what death was until you died, and then it was too late. Depression settled over me like a heavy fog. Death had struck close to me again, and I wondered whether Flint or I would be next. I didn't want to die, but I didn't really want to live either. Life wasn't a precious gift to me. I was born by accident. I'd be here a short time and then gone. I remembered the snowflakes and how quickly they melted. Maybe I was melting now and didn't know it. The more I tried to figure it out, the more senseless it became and the deeper I sank into the black well of depression.

The early spring wind was howling outside, and I paced the floor. I wanted to break loose and run, but there are no hills to run to in the city. Besides, people would think I was crazy or in some kind of trouble. No, I couldn't run with the wind tonight, but I could at least go for a walk. By the time I had walked a block, I was feeling a lot better. This was the first really warm spring evening we had had. There would soon be other warm evenings, but the first was special. I remembered how Grandmother used to go out on nights like this and put her ear to the ground. She would say she was listening for the first heartbeat of mother earth after she had slept the winter. When she was sure she had heard the earth's heartbeat she would say, "Mother earth is awake now. We can plant our garden soon."

The fresh air lifted me up out of the depression I had been living with. Without thinking much about where I was going I

88

found myself only a block away from the church. I stopped on the street corner trying to decide whether to go on to the church and see Reverend McPherson or to turn back and go home. I stood there while the traffic light changed several times and finally decided to walk past the church. He probably wouldn't be there anyway. Even if he was, there would probably be some kind of service going on. I wasn't sure when the church services were or what kind they were, but I sure wasn't going to get involved in anything like that.

In a few minutes I was standing in front of the church. The building was dark except for the study. It was brightly lighted, and I could see Reverend McPherson sitting at his desk reading. He was alone.

I walked up the steps, went inside, and knocked on his door.

"Come in," he said. I heard him push his chair away from his desk. I opened the door part way. When he saw me, he stood up and smiled.

"Come in. I was hoping you would come and visit us."

"Are you busy?" I asked, still hanging onto the doorknob.

"No. Come in and talk awhile. How are you?" He sat back down and motioned to a chair for me.

I sat on the edge of the chair.

"My uncle killed himself," I said abruptly. I surprised myself because I hadn't meant to say that at all.

"I'm sorry to hear that. Is there anything I can do?" he asked.

"No." I sat there quietly for a moment.

Then I looked him straight in the eyes and asked, "What happens when we die?"

"A lot of things. It depends on what kind of life you led here on earth and whether or not you knew Christ and what you did about it." He leaned forward in his chair.

"Who is Christ?" I asked. "You talked about God and about

89

Jesus and now you have a new person named Christ. Do you have three Gods?"

He smiled. "There is God, the Father and Creator of all things, and his only Son, Jesus Christ, Our Lord, and there is the Holy Spirit."

"Yes, three Gods."

"No, they are called the holy Trinity, three in one."

"I don't understand."

"It's not easy to understand. It is something far beyond the touch of our small, human minds, but you don't have to understand something completely to believe in it. Anyway, that's not what I'd like to get into tonight. I want to answer your question about what happens when a person dies."

"I guess I already know. When you die, you die, and your body rots," I said. I could almost hear Grandmother's voice again. I wondered if my eyes had the same look of fear in them that hers had had.

"That would be terribly sad if that were true. Man is too precious to die the same, hopeless way a dog dies. You see, human beings have souls, and that makes the difference. Man can choose between right and wrong. He can choose to accept God or reject Him. He can choose heaven or hell."

"Those are only church words; they don't mean anything to me. You can't say for a fact what happens to a person when he dies," I argued, feeling strangely stubborn.

"Yes, I can. God knew that man was afraid of death. He knew there would be questions in a man's heart, so He gave us answers. In fact, the very question you just asked me tonight was asked thousands of years ago by a man named Job. He cried out, 'If a man die, shall he live again?' "

"Once a man dies, he can't live again. The Kickapoo prophet said that when he died, he would be raised up again, but he wasn't. He just stayed dead. Dead is dead," I said.

90

"But that's the miracle of it! Man not only lives again, but he can live forever! This life is short and full of trouble and heartache and pain. If the next life were like this one, no one would want to live forever. But the next life will be beautiful if you are a believer. There will be love and peace and no tears and no death. We will live in a beautiful place that God has made especially for us. I can't find words to describe the joy I feel in my heart when I think of what lies ahead for us!" His eyes sparkled.

"How do you know?"

"The Bible says so," he said and put his hand on his ragged, frayed Bible.

"The Bible doesn't mean anything to me. It is only a book."

He settled back into his chair. "Yes, I see the problem you are having. I always take it for granted that people accept the Bible as the divine word of God. And I forget that there are many people who have never even seen a Bible." He looked at me. "Do you own a Bible?"

"No." I shook my head. "There's no reason for me to own a Bible. Do you own a war drum?"

He laughed, and so did I for the first time in a week.

"No, I don't own a war drum, but I do have a Bible I can give you. Then you'll be one up on me."

Before I could think of a reason for him not to give me one, he had gone to a shelf of his library and pulled out a Bible and written my name on it.

"Here, now this belongs to Crying Wind." He handed it to me.

"You shouldn't have put my name on it. Someone else might want it."

I have other Bibles I can give other people. This one is special; it is just for you."

I reached out and took it. As soon as my fingers curled around

91

the hard, black cover, I felt as if I had taken a step, made some sort of an unspoken commitment. I didn't know to whom or to what, but I knew that when I accepted that Bible, things weren't going to be the same. It was too late to give it back to him; my name had been written on the inside cover. Like it or not, I now owned a Bible.

"But what about the medicine man? They have power to do things," I said.

"Yes, I'm sure they do. I believe the devil gives them power so they can fool the people into believing the wrong things."

"But if Christians have power, and the devil gives other people power, how do you know who is right?"

"Because power from God always leads to good and power from the devil will always lead to destruction."

We talked about another hour. My mind seemed to be swirling with words and ideas that were new and strange to me. Some sort of mystery was unfolding, but I didn't understand any of it.

It was getting late, so I thanked him for his time and for the book he had given me.

"Don't be discouraged if you feel a little lost in what we talked about tonight. The wisest men in the world are confused about death and about the next life. It's probably the deepest subject you'll ever talk or think about. It takes time to understand it, but one of these days it will all fall into place for you, and you'll understand everything." He shook my hand. "Just remember that there is an answer to every question, and we can know for a certainty what lies beyond the grave."

I didn't answer as I opened the door.

"Don't stay away too long," he said.

"I don't think I'll be back. I don't believe what you say," I replied.

I expected him to be angry, but instead he only looked sad.

"If you change your mind you can always find me here," he said softly.

I turned my back on him and walked away. I wished he hadn't given me that book, the one with *Holy Bible* written on it in gold letters.

As I walked home in the dark I kept saying to myself, *Stupid! I was stupid to go there tonight!* I felt depressed again, and an overwhelming loneliness swept over me. *What if he was right? What if there was another life after death?* When I got home, I shoved the Bible into a drawer. Tomorrow I would throw it away. I just wished he hadn't written my name on it.

I felt as if there were a raging fire hidden just beneath the surface of my skin. I wanted to smash things, to scream and yell. I wanted to kill my enemies and hold their scalps in my hands and scream to the skies that I had met my enemy and I had killed him and I was the victor! Oh, if only I could have lived a hundred years ago. Life would have been simple. If you hated someone, you killed him. You were not punished; you were praised because you had defeated your enemy. *Life made more sense then,* I thought. *Who was my enemy? Everybody,* I thought gloomily, and threw a pillow across the room.

I was on the warpath all the next week. I didn't speak to anyone unless I had to. At work I just tried to fade into the background as much as possible. I ate my lunch alone in the back of a dusty storeroom instead of joining the others in the lunchroom upstairs. As I walked to and from work, I kept my eyes on the ground and refused to even look at the sky or the trees or anything around me. I was angry, but I wasn't sure why.

On Friday afternoon as I was leaving work, I saw Flint waiting outside for me. He was leaning against the side of the building and didn't see me until I was beside him.

I was never so happy to see anyone in my life.

93

"Waiting for someone?" I asked. I could feel the depression and anger of the past week falling away from me like a blanket.

"Yeah," he said casually and straightened up. "I'm looking for a skinny, ugly Kickapoo squaw. Have you seen any around?"

"No, but if I see one I'll let you know." I laughed. "I'm glad to see you."

"I didn't have anything else to do," he said and started walking down the street.

I fell into step beside him. "What goes?"

"I heard about a sing out west of town tonight. I thought you might like to go with me if you didn't have any plans."

I tried to hold back my excitement. "Sounds good. I didn't have any plans." I never had any plans. I was sure Flint knew that and was just trying to make me feel good.

"I'll buy you some supper, and then we'll head out that way. Heard there is going to be a lot there. It's just for bloods," he said and climbed into his pickup.

By "bloods" he meant it was just for Indians, and it was closed to the "no bloods" which meant white people. I was glad he didn't say anything about "mix-bloods," which is what I was. It was just a polite term for half-breed.

As we drove down the long stretch of highway, Flint kept increasing his speed until I knew he must be doing eighty miles an hour. He was talking and laughing. He seemed happier than I had seen him in a long time. Soon I could feel my spirits lifting, too. I rolled down my window and let the fresh summer air blow against my face. I no longer felt tired; the wind was blowing new strength into my body.

The moon was full and the color of Navajo silver. It was almost as bright as day. I could see every fence post beside the road and every tree and horse we passed.

I felt good. I was glad Flint had asked me to come with him. I let out a long sigh and leaned back in the seat. This was the way to be—free and with someone who was like you. I didn't need a new religion and a new way of life. This was where I belonged; with my own people on our way to a sing.

The faster Flint drove, the more miles he put between myself and my empty apartment and Reverend McPherson and his church. If Flint drove fast enough, I was sure I could leave everything behind, even the new God I had heard about.

Flint talked steadily, but I only heard part of what he was saying. I was caught up in the moonlight and the speed of the pickup and my own thoughts. My mind went back to the special ride I had had on Thunder Hooves. I felt a pang of loneliness and loss, knowing that some part of my life was over forever.

Flint slowed the truck down and turned onto a narrow dirt road. I sat up and looked around.

"It's only a few more miles," he said, and then he was quiet as he concentrated on the narrow, twisting road. He hit some ruts, and the wheels jerked hard. He slowed down a little more.

I could feel the mood of the evening slipping away. I tried to hang onto it. I looked over at Flint and saw that he wasn't smiling anymore.

I began wishing we had missed the turnoff. I wished we could have kept driving for hours and hours. I knew it was already too late to recapture the mood I had felt earlier, so I stopped trying and watched the road, which had turned into more of a trail than a road.

Flint slammed on the brakes. I was thrown forward but managed to put my hands against the dashboard and catch myself just before my head banged against the windshield.

"What's wrong?" I couldn't see any reason for him to stop.

"Up there, those rocks," he said and made a sharp left turn.

A pile of three rocks was visible by the headlights, one rock on top of another beside the road. No one would have noticed them. Even if someone had, he wouldn't have known the rocks were a signal to leave the road and cut across country if he hadn't known the silent language of trail signs.

We had bumped across about a half mile of sagebrush and rocks, when we saw more than a dozen pickups and cars parked in a corral of scrub oak and giant tumbleweeds. The first people to arrive had made a rough, horseshoe-shaped corral, about four feet high and large enough to allow parking for about fifteen cars and trucks. In the old days, horses would have been kept there during the pow-wow. Tonight the corral's purpose was to conceal the cars and trucks from outsiders. No one was welcome here who wasn't invited.

Before dawn, after the ceremonies, everyone would leave quietly and quickly, a few at a time, fading away into the darkness. The fire would be carefully put out and the ashes buried. The corral would be taken down and the bushes and tumbleweeds scattered. By dawn there would be no trace that anyone had been here tonight. Unlike the white man who left empty cans and cigarette butts and candywrappers behind, the Indians left nothing behind, often not even their footprints.

Flint shut off the motor. We got out of the truck and quietly shut the doors. Then he took the lead, and I followed him through the underbrush and up the steep hill until we reached the rim of the canyon.

Between us and the rim of the canyon were four dancers standing in a line beside the campfire. Beyond the dancers was only blackness that stretched from the Canyon of the Old Dead Ones up into the starless sky.

I followed Flint and sat down beside him in the circle of Indians who were seated on the ground. Most of them were wrapped in blankets. I looked around for a familiar face, but they were all strangers to me. I could see by the different jewelry and blanket designs that three different tribes were represented. I was so absorbed in watching the others that I was startled when

96

The shrill, anguished cry of the dancers pierced the air.

the shrill anguished cry of the dancers pierced the silence. I quickly turned my attention to the four dancers as they moved around the fire. Each step was measured and exact, just as the dance had been danced a thousand years ago on this same canyon rim by our ancestors. Their shrill cries imitating the coyote god were so successful that coyotes wailed in the distance.

Suddenly I shivered with chill bumps, and the back of my neck tingled. I inched closer to my uncle. He handed me his jacket. I pulled it tightly around my shoulders.

The dancers were moving faster. I felt as if my own heart were keeping rhythm with the drum. I had always thrilled at the sound of Indian drums, but tonight it sounded threatening and evil, as if it were stealing something from me. Most of the other Indians had joined in the chant. Their bodies were swaying in time to the drumbeat. It was as if we were all going into a trance.

Then I saw it beside the dancers! A thin white, almost transparent smoke. It was small at first, but it grew larger and larger until it was as tall as a man. It was spinning around like a dust devil. It had no shape or substance. I was frightened, but I couldn't take my eyes off of it. I sensed that it was evil and dangerous. I wanted to speak or move, but I felt numb. As the dance ended, the white whirlwind grew smaller and smaller and finally disappeared. When it was gone, I turned to Flint.

"What was that?" I whispered.

"What?" He leaned over to hear me better, but his eyes were still watching the fire.

He hadn't seen it or he wouldn't have had to ask what I was talking about.

"Never mind. It was nothing," I said and looked back at the glowing fire. I must have imagined it. There hadn't really been anything there or Flint would have seen it, too. But why did I feel so strange inside? I was glad I had Flint's jacket on so he couldn't see me shaking. I wished the dances would end. I wanted to go home. There was something not right here in the Canyon of the Old Dead Ones!

I sat quietly through two more hours of dances. I wanted to leave, but I was afraid to complain because Flint might not ask me to go anywhere with him again. I tried to think about other things because I didn't want to see the white whirling thing again. I kept telling myself that maybe I was just tired, or maybe it had been a shadow, but I couldn't convince myself that I hadn't really seen it, so I avoided looking at the dancers or the fire or the rim of the canyon and kept my eyes on the toes of my moccasins and the ground around me. Countless times I caught myself thinking about Reverend McPherson and how it felt to be inside the church. There had been no white, whirling things in the church. I would ask him about that when I saw him next time; he would know what it was. Then I remembered that I had told him I wouldn't be back. I had made a bad mistake by ever talking to him or going to that church. Maybe tonight was a warning not ever to stray from the Old Way again. Yes, that must be it. I belonged here. These were my people; these were my gods they were singing about. But I didn't feel a part of things.

Flint sat motionless, completely lost in the movements of the dancers and the chants. He belonged here. He was part of this, but he didn't look happy. I glanced around the circle. No one was smiling; all the dark faces looked like carved stone. I guess an Indian doesn't have any reason to smile.

The last dance came to an end. There was nothing to signal that this was the end of the evening. The dancers simply walked off into the darkness, the drum stopped, people stood up and silently faded into the shadows.

I stood up and brushed the dust off myself.

"Come on, Flint," I said and tugged on his arm. "It's over. Let's get out of here."

He stood up and stretched. "No, I think I'll stick around," he said and nodded his head toward a clump of trees.

I turned to see what he meant. My heart sank. Hidden among the trees was a tipi. That tipi meant only one thing. There was going to be a peyote ceremony here tonight.

I hadn't seen it when we arrived. It must have been hastily erected sometime during the dances. Flint probably hadn't come here expecting a peyote ceremony or he wouldn't have asked me to come along. Now that he knew one would be held, he wanted to stay for it.

99

"Please, Flint," I pleaded and held onto his arm more tightly.

"I'm going to stay for the peyote ceremony," he said in a voice that wouldn't allow for any arguments from me. He pulled his arm free. We stood there in a deadlock, neither of us speaking.

I looked down at the ground and dug my heels into the soft earth.

He reached into the pocket of his Levis and took out the keys to the pickup.

"Look, kid. You take these and go wait in the truck. I won't be long."

I took the keys and started toward the truck. My throat hurt and my eyes burned. I turned around hoping he had changed his mind and I would see him following me, but he was already at the entrance of the tipi.

I walked back to the truck and climbed inside. It would serve him right if I just drove off and left him here.

I stuck the key in the ignition and slid behind the steering wheel. I sat there wanting to leave but unable to make myself drive off and leave him. He had known when he handed me the keys that I would be sitting here waiting for him when he came back.

I buried my head in my hands and cried. I cried because I was angry with Flint and the world. I cried because what had started out as a special evening had turned sour and because I was alone again. No matter where I went or what I did, I always ended up alone.

I laid down in the seat of the pickup and cried until I heard the drum begin to beat inside the tipi. I sat up and wiped my tears off on my sleeve and watched the tipi. Smoke was coming out the top—the ceremony was beginning. Even though I was never allowed to go to a peyote ceremony, I knew exactly what was going on inside the tipi just as well as if I were sitting inside next to Flint.

Peyote is a cactus that grows in the southwest. When it is eaten it is supposed to increase the senses. It dulls the consciousness and takes a person to a half-dream world where he can see visions and speak to the spirits. To the Indian, peyote represents the mother earth. According to legend, a long time ago a woman was alone and dying. She heard a voice that told her to eat a plant that was growing nearby. When she had eaten it, she was strong enough to find her way back to her tribe. She taught them how to have peyote ceremonies.

Most Indians call the peyote ritual "half-moon way," so that non-Indians won't know what they are talking about.

I saw the flap pulled shut over the entrance of the tipi. Everything had to be exact for the ceremony. The entrance was facing east. Four Indian men conducted the ceremony. The roadman is the leader, then the drummer chief, the cedar chief, and the fire chief. To begin, the roadman stands in the center of the tipi, faces west, and lies down on the ground. He does this to rid himself of his pride and humble himself on mother earth's breast. He stretches his arms outward as far as he can and uses his fingertips to draw a half circle in the dirt to form the half moon. Then he draws a line along the top of the moon called the peyote road, or the road of life. The roadman sits opposite the entrance and the drummer chief sits at his right. The drum is a special one for peyote rites. It is made by filling a metal drum one-fourth full of water and stretching a wet deerskin over it. To the left of the roadman sits the cedar chief. He sprinkles cedar on the sacred fire during the night-long ceremony. The fire chief sits at the entrance of the tipi and cares for the fire and keeps outsiders from entering.

The sacred fire is built by placing pieces of wood in the shape of a V with the open top of the V facing east and the closed end facing the west. The other firewood is also laid in a special way.

Sage is placed throughout the tipi. Flint and the other Indians would be sitting on piles of sage.

After everyone is settled, the fire chief sprinkles cedar on the fire and is given the single eagle feather that gives him authority over anyone entering or leaving the tipi.

Everyone removes his clothing except the four men in charge. They rub their arms, chest and body with sage to cleanse themselves. Sage has always been a healing plant. It is also a spirit plant that can drive away evil spirits.

When the peyote buttons are brought out and passed around,

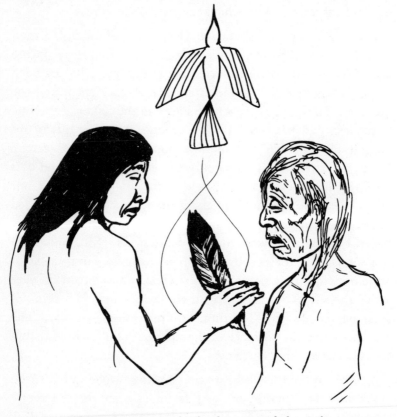

The roadman passes his feathers around the circle.

102

all the men take four each. Then the roadman takes "father peyote" from his beaded ritual box, holds it over the smoke from the sacred fire, and puts it in front of himself. The peyote button used for the father is a large, perfectly formed button. Sometimes an altar is made from buckskin or a beaded cloth and this peyote button is placed on it.

Other ceremonial objects are placed around father peyote, a whistle made from an eagle bone, a branch of sage, a gourd rattle with a specially beaded handle (peyote beadwork is different from other beadwork), an arrow, and the roadman's personal peyote feathers. He uses eagle feathers if he can get them. If he can't, he uses trimmed turkey feathers.

Then the roadman picks up the sage branch and an eagle feather in his left hand and the gourd rattle in his right hand and begins to chant a peyote song. The drum chief begins to play the drum. Each chant is sung four times. Four is a sacred number to Indians; it represents the four directions and the four seasons. Then the roadman passes his gourd and feathers and sage around the circle and some of the men take turns singing. If they don't want to sing, they pass it to the next man.

I wondered if Flint ever sang. I doubted it. I didn't think he wanted to participate in anything as much as he wanted to escape from everything.

At midnight more cedar was added to the fire, the midnight water chant is sung four times, and a pail of water is brought inside the tipi. Then Flint and the others eat the peyote buttons and drink the water. They keep at it until dawn.

I could guess almost exactly what Flint was doing, but there was no way I could tell what kind of visions he was having. They might be good or bad. They might be about death and evil spirits, or the visions might be good medicine that would give him strength and help.

I knew he had used peyote many times before. He didn't

talk much about it, but it seemed that the more anyone used it, the more he needed to use it.

The steady beat of the drum and boredom of sitting alone in the truck finally put me to sleep. I woke several times during the night. I could see the moon had moved far across the sky, and it would soon be morning. Each time I woke, I still heard the drum beating.

Just as the eastern sky was faintly lighted by the false dawn, I woke again and stretched my stiff, aching body. I was tired, hungry, and thirsty. My neck hurt from sleeping in a crooked position.

I saw the morning water woman approach the tipi with a pail of water. She is usually a woman who is related to the roadman. She is invited inside to smoke some cornhusk and pray, then she gives everyone a drink of water from her pail and leaves, taking the water with her. Then she stands outside the tipi and passes in the four sacred foods; water, corn, nuts, and meat. These represent the life the Indians had before the appearance of the white man. Everyone inside the tipi eats some of the food. After all this, the sacred peyote objects are put away, the ritual box is closed, and the ceremony is over.

I watched the tipi entrance for Flint to come out. Two other men came out before he did. One of them laid down near a small tree and held onto it with both hands as if he thought the earth was shaking and he was going to fall off. The other man took only a few steps and became ill and vomited. As Flint stumbled toward the truck, I knew he wouldn't be able to drive. I opened the door on my side and slid over to the driver's seat and motioned to him. I hoped he wouldn't get sick or pass out. He had to try three times before he could climb into the truck. His eyes were glassy and red, his lips looked swollen and parched, but he was smiling and singing to himself. He hardly knew I was there. I started the motor and hoped I would be able to find my way back to the highway. There was no point in asking Flint for any help with directions in the condition he was in. I got lost twice and had to backtrack, but I finally reached the highway and headed for home.

During the drive the night before, time and miles had passed swiftly. Today in the harsh daylight, I was tired and the miles seemed to drag. A couple of times I tried to talk to Flint, but he couldn't really hear me or understand anything I said. He sang peyote songs and talked about wild horses and flying on a huge bird, just bits and pieces of medicine dreams he had had.

I wanted to get home before the effects of the peyote wore off. I had seen people go through this before. For a few hours afterwards they were happy and peaceful. When the peyote wore off, they went down, down into a deep dark hole of black depression and stayed there for hours or even days.

Flint would fight the depression by getting drunk. That was followed by a hangover, and then depression, and then peyote. And the circle of death would start over again. We were both caught in the circle. *There is no way out of a circle,* I thought. My head felt dizzy, and before I knew it, I had driven off the road. My tires hit the loose gravel along side the pavement. I gave the wheel a sudden twist and jerked the pickup back onto the highway and slowed down. My hands were sweating. I'd nearly had an accident. We could have turned over and been killed. *You die.* I thought. *That's how you get out of the circle.* I glanced over at Flint, but he wasn't even awake enough to know what had happened.

I sat up straighter in the seat and opened my window to get some cold air on my face. Had I just been tired and had that near wreck been just an accident, or had it been something else?

Chapter Eight

I felt like I was walking into a steel trap as I walked through the doors of the department store to start another day at work. I hung up my coat and tried to shut off my mind and not think about anything except the countless customers who would trail in and out of the store all day. There was new stock to be put away. As I began taking the china out of the crate, I looked at the price list. One teacup twelve dollars, one plate was eighteen dollars, and a complete set of this china came to hundreds of dollars. I thought of the cracked, chipped, mismatched dishes Grandmother and I had used. "Oh well," I said to myself, "An eighteen dollar plate doesn't hold any more fry bread and beans than a ten cent plate from the trading post." But these people didn't eat fry bread and beans. They ate strange, expensive foods. They even ate fish! I shuddered. Grandmother had always told me that our people would never eat fish because fish contained the souls of dead women who had been evil during their lifetime.

I'd just finished putting up the last of the china on the shelves when Betty walked over and handed me a piece of paper and a pencil. "Would you like to sign this?" she asked.

"What is it?"

"Mrs. Montgomery, who works in the drygoods department, is retiring this week. Everyone in the store is signing this paper. We'll put it in a nice card for her. She's worked in this store in the drygoods department fifty years. She started when she was only fifteen years old." Betty shook her head. "Can you imagine that? Fifty years in this place. Boy, I sure won't be working here fifty years. As soon as I find the right man, I'm getting married and getting out of here." She waited for me to sign the paper and then she left. I heard her say again, "Fifty years!"

I thought about Mrs. Montgomery. She was my age when she started working here and she had stayed, stayed all her life. Every day she saw the same things and the same people, everything always the same—

A customer walked over and picked up one of the teacups I had just put on display.

"May I help you?" I asked.

She looked up and her face went into a frown. "If you don't mind, I would rather have someone else wait on me."

I felt as if a bucket of ice water had been thrown on me. I turned and went after Betty. I tried to sound casual, but I knew the stiffness of my smile and the tremor in my voice gave me away as I said, "Betty, would you mind waiting on that lady over there?"

"Sure, but I thought you were taking care of her," she said, glancing at the lady.

"She asked for someone else." I shrugged my shoulders. "Maybe her great-great-grandfather was scalped by Indians." I turned my back toward the customer and finished marking prices on merchandise while Betty made the sale. The customer left, and Betty hurried back to my side.

"Don't let her bother you. She's the kind of person who doesn't like anybody."

The morning dragged by, and it was finally time for lunch. I didn't feel like I could face another lunch from my brown paper bag. I felt empty, but I wasn't hungry. I stood around a few minutes trying to decide what to do with the next hour if I didn't eat lunch. Maybe some fresh air might clear my head. I hadn't had much sleep last night. I was probably just tired, and a walk would perk me up and give me an appetite.

The second I opened the door, I knew I had made the right

decision. The fresh air and sunshine made me feel good after being in the old, stuffy building. I began to walk away from the store, and with each step I felt better. I walked for blocks and blocks, not caring where I was going as long as I could get away from the store for awhile. Suddenly I came upon a small park. It was only a single square block, but it was like finding a wilderness in the middle of concrete and steel city. I sat down on the soft grass and looked at the trees and flowers. I wished I was back on the reservation where I could walk on the earth and not the hard pavement and where coyotes were heard crying at night instead of traffic on the streets.

I hadn't been sitting there very long when a man in a uniform came up to me and said, "I'm sorry, miss. You aren't allowed to sit on the grass."

I stood up.

He smiled. "What I meant was, people aren't allowed on the grass. You're supposed to stay on the little pathways." He pointed to several winding cement paths.

I was embarrassed, and my face felt hot. I didn't speak or look at him as I left the park. Always, always they want you to walk on the hard cement. Don't touch the grass. Don't feel the softness of mother earth beneath your feet.

Nearly an hour had passed as I came within sight of the store again. My lunch hour would be over in a few more minutes, but as I came to the store, my feet kept going. I didn't stop at the door; I just kept walking. I wouldn't go back there. I couldn't go back there. No more time spent in the steel trap. I wouldn't spend fifty years there! I remembered my coat still being inside, but I wouldn't go back even to get that. "Good-bye, coat," I said and kept walking in the direction of home.

Without a job, time passed slowly. I was bored and restless and longed for something to do. When Sunday came, I was so desperate I decided to go to church. What harm could it do?

108

Trinity Evangelical United Brethren Church

My knees shook as I climbed up the steps and entered the church. I stood just inside the doorway, unsure whether to go inside or turn and run back down the steps. My decision was made for me as some other people came through the door behind me, and I had to move ahead to get out of their way.

A few more uncertain steps found me inside the main part of the church. Light streamed in through the stained-glass windows with pictures on them. One window showed a man with some sheep. Another window showed men sitting at a table eating together.

My knees were shaking so badly now that I had to sit down. I didn't know where to go. Perhaps special people had special seats on these long benches with the high backs. Perhaps there was no place for me to sit at all. The other people walked around me and found places to sit toward the front of the room, so I followed them and slipped into the third row and clung to the edge of the seat.

Soft music seemed to come from nowhere, and I heard voices singing songs I didn't understand.

My heart was pounding so hard I was sure other people could hear it. I wondered if all the people were looking at me and wondering what I was doing in their church. I sat frozen and terrified. Any moment I was sure someone would see me and ask me to leave. Perhaps they would all stand up and point their fingers at me and shout at me and chase me away! I wished I hadn't come here. I didn't belong; I wasn't part of these people. I kept my eyes on my hands knotted tightly in my lap. I was afraid I was going to do something wrong and call attention to myself.

After a while a man handed a flat plate to me with money on it. I looked at him and then back at the plate. My stomach had a sick feeling in it as I held the plate. What was I supposed to do with this?

The man smiled and leaned down and whispered, "Would you please pass that down the row for me?"

How stupid I felt! I handed it to the person next to me so suddenly she almost dropped it. I could feel my neck getting hot, and I felt like running away. I had to get out of this building and back where I belonged! I gathered my courage and stood up to leave. Suddenly everyone in the entire church stood up, too!

I was so startled I didn't move. Were all these people going to stop me from leaving?

Then Reverend McPherson appeared at the front of the church.

I let out a sigh of relief. He wouldn't let these people hurt me. He would let me get away!

He said a few words, and all the people bowed their heads as if they were ashamed. Then he said a few more words and everyone sat down. Without thinking, I sat back down, too.

I kept my eyes on Reverend McPherson. He was talking again about this man named Jesus. I wondered what Grand-

110

mother would say if she knew I was in a white man's prayer house. I didn't think she would like it.

Soon the end of church had come, and everyone was leaving the building. A few people stopped and shook my hand and told me their names and asked me mine, but I didn't tell them. Didn't these foolish people know that if an Indian says his own name out loud three times in the same hour his ears will wither up? *White people have so much to learn,* I thought.

Reverend McPherson was at the door shaking hands with people as they left. I timidly put out my hand and he smiled as he held it firmly in his.

"We are all so happy to have you here today. Can you stay and eat lunch with us?"

I hadn't expected this and didn't know what to say. The red-haired woman standing beside him stepped forward and slipped her arm around my shoulder.

"I'm Mrs. McPherson. You call me Audrey. We would be so happy if you would eat with us." Then, almost as if she had read my mind, she added, "After you've eaten you can stay as long as you like or leave whenever you want."

"All right." I agreed and followed them next door to their home.

It only took her a few minutes to have everything ready and on the table.

"We always thank God for our food," Reverend McPherson said. He and Audrey both bowed their heads, closed their eyes, and talked to their God for a minute.

Then Audrey reached over and took the lid off a covered dish.

I had to swallow hard to keep from choking. It was fish! A long fish with eyes that looked right at me and made my skin crawl.

"How much would you like?" Reverend McPherson asked.

111

"I—can't eat that—fish. She is looking at me!"

"I'm not hungry," I said weakly, unable to take my eyes off the eyes of the fish.

"Is anything wrong?" Audrey asked.

I started to repeat that I just wasn't hungry, but at the same second my stomach growled so loudly I knew they couldn't help but hear it.

"I—I can't eat that—fish. She is looking at me!" I said.

"She?" Audrey asked and leaned over for a closer look at the fish.

I felt miserable; this just wasn't my day. "My people believe that the spirits of evil women turn into fish. If we eat fish those spirits can live again in our bodies."

Without waiting a second more, Audrey covered the fish. I was glad her eyes were no longer looking at me. Audrey picked up the fish and carried it into the kitchen.

"I guess I will go now," I said and started to get up.

"We haven't eaten yet, and you must be hungry. Are their any legends about ham sandwiches?" Reverend McPherson asked with a twinkle in his eye.

"No, there are no spirits in ham sandwiches," I laughed.

The strangeness between us was melting away. We talked about many things. I could never remember laughing so much or talking so much.

The afternon was gone in a flash.

"Why don't you stay for dinner and go to the evening service at church?" Audrey suggested.

"Do you have church at night, too?" I asked. "Isn't that too often to talk to your God? Maybe He doesn't like to be bothered so much with people. Maybe He would rather sleep."

"Our God never sleeps," she said.

"Then He must get awfully tired. Even the wind sleeps sometimes," I said.

"Our God never gets tired. He is always eager to talk to us and hear our prayers."

I thought about that for a moment. "Is night church like morning church?"

"No, not exactly. There are not so many people there and it is more informal."

"Does that plate get passed around?" I asked.

"No. That's only in the morning service." Audrey laughed.

"What are you supposed to do with that plate anyway?" I asked.

"It's passed around so people who want to can put money in it to help support God's church and His work."

"I don't have any money," I said. "I didn't put any in the plate this morning. How much do I owe you for going to church?"

"Going to church is free. No one ever has to pay or give money if they don't want to. God is happy when people come, even if—especially if—they don't have any money."

"We'd like to have you stay," Audrey said.

I hesitated, and Reverend McPherson said, "Please."

"Ok, I'll stay," I said. After all, it hadn't been too bad this morning once I'd gotten used to it.

It was a quiet service. Fewer people came, and the plate wasn't passed around. I stayed for awhile, and then I decided I was tired of hearing about Jesus again. It seemed to me like they could find something else to talk about, so I got up and left.

113

Audrey had a puzzled look on her face, but she smiled and lifted her hand slightly to wave good-bye.

For the next few days I did nothing, and then I realized I had only two dollars left. I would have to get a job now or go hungry. I knew I didn't want to work as a clerk again and have customers refuse to let me wait on them because my skin was a different color. No more of that! Maybe I could find a job where I wouldn't have to be with people, something I could do alone.

I checked the want ads in the newspaper and saw an ad for a night cleaning woman for an office building. It sounded perfect. I didn't even finish looking at the rest of the ads. I tore the address out of the newspaper and left.

I had expected a big, tall building with a dozen offices, but it was a small building with only six offices and an entrance lounge. After I told the receptionist I was there about the job, a middle-aged man in a black suit motioned me into his office.

"You look awfully young," he said first. "We were really looking for someone older."

"I'm eighteen," I said. I had told that lie so many times that I almost believed it myself. "I can work very hard. Maybe I can work faster because I'm young," I said hopefully.

He laughed. "It isn't a glamourous job. The salary is small and work is dirty. You would come in after nine at night and dust, vacuum, and empty wastebaskets, and do whatever cleanup was necessary. You would leave whenever you were finished. One night you might work two hours, and another night you might have to work five hours. It's not really a job for a young girl."

"It's just what I want. I would work hard," I said seriously. I was anxious to have a job where I would be hidden from the public.

He studied me for a moment and then stood up. "All right.

114

The job is yours. Come in at six tonight, and the lady will show you what to do. Starting tomorrow night, you'll be working alone."

Finally something was going my way! I was really glad the job had been so easy to get. I had dreaded going from one place to another, only to be turned down. This job would be perfect. I would be alone. My hours would depend on how fast I worked, and the work would be fairly easy. It seemed too good to be true.

I stopped by the church one night to say hello to the McPhersons and tell them about my job.

"That's a rough neighborhood. Be very careful," Reverend McPherson warned.

"We wish you had a job in the daytime," Audrey scolded. "You are too young to be out so late at night!"

"I'm not too young," I said. "I'm fifteen."

"Fifteen!" Audrey groaned. "I was worried enough about you when I thought you were eighteen. Now that I know you are only fifteen I feel like I should take you under my wings and protect you from the world. You are too young to be on your own. You are only a baby!"

"Well, I feel like I'm a hundred years old," I said jokingly. I could tell by the look on her face that she didn't think it was funny.

"It's a sad thing to miss your childhood and grow up too soon."

I had been working my new job three weeks. Each night I left my place about eight and walked to the office building. I arrived there about nine. Most nights I finished my work by midnight and was home again by one.

As I was on my way to work one night, I suddenly became aware of footsteps behind me. There weren't many people out walking this late at night, especially since all the stores and offices were closed. I don't know what alarmed me. Maybe it

115

was an age-old instinct for danger, but whatever it was, I quickened my steps slightly. When I heard the footsteps behind me become faster, I was sure I was being followed. There was no one else on the street, not even a passing car. It was still another block to the office building, and there was an alley between where I was now and the office building. I knew that if anything was going to happen, it would be when I walked past that alley. I tried to tell myself that it was probably just some harmless little old lady walking home from visiting a friend, and if I turned around to look I would see how foolish I was being. But I couldn't make myself turn around and look. I was afraid that what I would see behind me would frighten me so badly I would be paralyzed and helpless, so I just kept walking.

The entrance to the alley was just ahead of me. It looked like a big, black hole. The footsteps had started to gain on me! I waited until I was almost to the alley entrance, and then I broke into a dead run. I ran as fast as I could. I felt as if my feet were

The footsteps had started to gain on me! I ran as fast as I could.

116

flying above the pavement. At any moment I expected to be grabbed around my throat, but I didn't look back. I just kept running. As I ran I took the key out of my pocket and held it in my hand, ready to unlock the door as soon as I reached it. I leaped up two steps at a time, jammed the key into the lock, gave it a sharp twist and kicked the door open, and yanked the key out. I shoved the door shut behind me, slammed the bolt down, ran down the dark hallway into the first office, and shut that door behind me, too.

With my heart pounding and my legs shaking, I stood in the darkness. I listened to hear if anyone was trying to get the door open. There was nothing but silence.

Well, I thought, *it was probably just a little old lady after all, and she's wondering what kind of a fool young girl runs down the street at night.* But I didn't believe it, not for a minute. I stood there a few minutes longer, unable to move. I knew I should forget about it and start working, but I was afraid to turn on a light. If anyone was out there, a light would tell him which office I was in. Maybe he would try to break in, or maybe he would wait until I was through and on my way home—at midnight.

I was scared. I couldn't remember ever being so scared. I wanted help, and I only knew one person to call. I reached for the telephone and dialed the operator and asked her to get Reverend McPherson.

Please let him be home! Please let him be home! I repeated over and over to myself as his phone rang.

When he picked it up and I heard his voice, I nearly collapsed from relief. "This is Crying Wind," I said in a shaky voice. "Please, please come and get me. I'm afraid—I'm sure someone is following me. I'm in the office building now, but I'm afraid he is outside waiting for me."

"I'll be right there. I'll honk the horn when I drive up. Stay where you are!"

I heard him hang up but I didn't want to let go of the phone, so I still held it to my ear. "Please hurry!" I whispered into the phone even though no one was there to hear.

I tried to imagine how long it would take him. I tried to picture in my mind where he was. *By now he would be turning onto 30th Avenue. Now he would be at 29th Avenue, unless he had to stop for a red light. No, please let all the lights be green! Now 28th Avenue. Maybe I should call the police.* Maybe the man who followed me was gone now, or maybe he had somehow gotten into the building. Maybe he was going from room to room looking for me—my neck ached from the tension. I wondered if there was anything in the room I could use for a weapon. I was sick with fear. The only sound was my breathing, and then I found that I was unconsciously holding my breath so there was no sound at all. Then I thought I heard something. Was it a footstep? I strained to hear it again. It was a horn! It was about a block away! There again, closer! I let out the breath I had been holding. Now the horn honked out front. It took me about two seconds to get out of the building and into the car beside Reverend McPherson.

"Are you all right?" he asked as he pulled quickly away from the curb.

"Yes." I was shaking all over. "Yes, I'm all right. How did you get here so fast?"

"I guess I ran a couple of red lights and drove over the speed limit, but I think God will overlook it this time."

"Did you see anyone? I was sure someone was after me."

"I didn't see anyone, but that doesn't mean much. If there was someone after you, he wouldn't let anyone else see him. I think we should drive to the police station and make a report. If there is someone on the prowl tonight, it would be a good idea for the police to know about it. They could send a squad car out here to look around."

I laughed nervously. "But what if it wasn't anything? After all, nothing really happened."

"That's OK. The police don't mind, and there's no reason to take any chances. Better safe than sorry. We have a built in warning system that tells us when we're in danger, even if we can't see anything. I think you did the right thing to call me."

He drove to the police station, and we made a report. The police said they would take a look around that area.

"Would you like to stay with Audrey and me tonight? Maybe you'd feel safer," he offered. "You know you are welcome."

"No, I'll be fine. Thanks anyway."

"I wish you would get a daytime job—"

I didn't let him finish. "Don't worry. I'm going to call in the morning and quit! I'll never go through this again! I don't think I've ever been so terrified in my life. You know, I've always thought I could take care of myself until tonight. Tonight I felt helpless and so scared." I was still shaking.

"Then you've learned something important tonight—everybody needs somebody sometime, and we all need God all the time. Mankind was never meant to face anything alone. Maybe God allowed you to be frightened tonight to teach you not to try to depend only on your own resources. Audrey and I have been so worried about you working nights. She'll be glad to know you won't be working there anymore. It wasn't really the right job for you anyway. You need a job that has some kind of future for you. What would you really like to do?"

I shrugged my tired shoulders. "I don't know. I've never thought about it. As long as I can eat I guess I don't care." Just as he drove up in front of my apartment I asked, "Were you and Audrey really worried about me?"

119

"Of course we were," he said. He waited until I was safely inside of my apartment, and then he drove away.

I kept telling myself I wasn't afraid anymore, but I checked several times to make sure the door was locked. I left all the lights on all night.

I didn't understand the city or its dangers. At home the night hadn't been dangerous. When the moon was full and the wind was high, I would go out for a ride on Thunder Hooves. We would gallop up and down the dark valley and across the shadowy hills. I hadn't been afraid of the darkness. It hadn't bothered me that I couldn't see, because Thunder Hooves saw for me. Only the coyotes were out that late at night, and they wouldn't harm us. As I remembered the midnight rides and Thunder Hooves, a pain stabbed through my heart because I would never again go on one of those rides with her.

Here in the city I stayed behind locked doors at night because it wasn't safe for a lone girl to be out late after dark. Yet the city was supposed to be civilized. The country was the wilderness, but in the wilderness with the wild animals I had been safe! It didn't make sense.

I didn't sleep much that night as I thought about two things Reverend McPherson had said. I wondered why he thought I needed a job with a future. After all, it was plain I was nobody going nowhere. I had been lonely and unhappy all my life. I was that way now, and I knew the future held more of the same. Then I wondered why he and Audrey would worry about me. No one had ever worried about me before. Sometimes he said things that puzzled me, but one thing was sure, tonight I had asked him for help and he had come running.

It was back to the want ads again. One ad asked for someone to make pottery, and my hopes soared. If there was one thing an Indian could do it was make pottery!

120

I hurried to the address. As soon as I walked into the office I said, "I've come to get the job making pottery."

"Fine. Fine. Have you ever worked with pottery before?" asked the lady as she handed me the forms to fill out.

"Well, my grandmother knew how, and when I was a small girl she showed me how to make pottery, but it was a long time ago. I've forgotten a lot of what she taught me, but maybe it would come back."

"That's OK. We'll train you to fit in. Follow me," she said and turned down a long hall. I walked closely behind her. She stopped at two large, heavy doors with little glass windows in them.

I looked beyond her and through the windows and caught a glimpse of huge machines and pipes going from one to another. As soon as she opened the door, the most deafening noise I had ever heard in my life made me instinctively put my hands over my ears to shut out the sound.

She looked at me and laughed. "Haven't you ever worked in a factory before?"

I could hardly hear her above the noise, but I shook my head.

"It's all right. You will get used to the noise, and you won't notice it at all."

I felt as if there were a thousand drums beating in my head. How could anyone get used to that?

She pointed at a long row of switches and levers. "This is what you will operate. You will be told when to punch the switches or move the levers. You must not do anything unless that man in the apron over there tells you. It all depends on times and temperatures and the thickness of the clay for the pottery. He will tell you all you need to know. Just do exactly as he tells you." She waved at the man in the apron, and he came over to explain my job to me.

121

I stood there pushing, pulling, and punching. The noise seemed to grind its way into the center of my mind. I tried to shut it out by thinking of other things. I remembered how Grandmother showed me how Indians made pottery in the old days. She would take a little gourd, fill it with water, pour it on the ground, and get down on her hands and knees and watch the water soak in the ground. Then she would add a little more water and say, "Now you must be gentle, for you are scratching skin from the breast of mother earth." She would dig into the mud with her fingers and take the wet earth in her hands. She formed it and worked it and re-formed it until it became a small, uneven bowl. When she was satisfied with it, she would put it on a tree stump to dry in the sun. The hot summer sun would bake it hard as stone. It was a simple, natural way to make pottery, using mother earth and water and sun. It had been quiet, not noisy like this place. I wished I could once more be back scraping the mud into my hands with Grandmother.

Far down the line a machine was stamping a design on some of the finished pottery. Stamp. Stamp. Stamp. Each one alike. I remembered seeing Indian women painting their pottery by hand, using yucca brushes that had only three or four bristles. It took them hours and sometimes even days to finish painting one bowl. They were proud of their work. There was no pride in this.

I closed my eyes and curled my fingers, aching to feel mud from that day so long ago. Instead my fingers curled around a cold, steel lever. I opened my eyes and looked around. This was not the way to make pottery. This was not the way for an Indian to live.

I pushed the heavy doors open and walked down that long hall and outside the building. It was quiet outside. My head stopped pounding with the noise of machines. I reached down beside me and scraped a small piece of dirt up between my

122

fingers. Mother earth was still here. It was the same mother earth as back on the reservation. Why did everything seem so different here?

I walked home. This job had lasted two hours. What was wrong with me? Why couldn't I just go to work and put in the time and go home like other people? Why did I remember the past? Why did I think about mother earth and the sun and the seasons?

As I was walking home, a car honked behind me and pulled over to the curb. I turned around and looked. Audrey and Reverend McPherson were motioning for me to come over to the car.

"We saw you walking and wanted to know if you had any luck job hunting today," Audrey said.

"Yes, I found a job. I worked two hours," I told her as I leaned against the door of the car.

"Two hours? What happened?"

"I quit."

There was a mixture of amusement and disappointment on her face.

"What now?" she asked.

"I don't know," I answered.

"Dear child!" she said. "You can't spend the rest of your life changing jobs every few weeks. You need a purpose, a plan, some kind of goal for yourself. Isn't there anything you want in life?"

"No, I guess not." I stood up and walked away from the car.

"Can we give you a ride home? You look tired."

"No, I think I'll walk."

"Is there anything we can do to help you?" she asked.

I didn't answer this time. I just shook my head and walked away.

The wind had come up. It made me feel cool and relaxed. After I got home, I opened all the windows to let the wind blow fresh air into the apartment. I got out some beads and began working on a necklace, looking up sometimes to watch the curtains blowing back and forth. I worked until dark. My eyes were so tired I went to bed and watched the stars out of my window. The stars seemed smaller here, farther away. It was not like back home, where you could almost touch the stars, where they were just a little higher than the mountain peaks.

The wind had become very strong just before dawn, and the curtains had blown against the lamp beside my bed and knocked it over. It woke me up. I got up and started to close the window and go back to bed, but the sight of the black, shadowy tree limbs being tossed back and forth by the wind caught my attention. I stood at the window, watching the wind play with the trees.

When I did crawl back into bed, I noticed my cheeks were wet from tears. I hadn't even known I was crying.

"Oh, if only I could go back home—if only I could go back home—" I whispered to myself, over and over.

Chapter Nine

As the wind blew louder, I could hear his voice calling me, calling me back home, back to the reservation, back home to the hills and valleys I knew and longed for.

I grabbed a pillow, yanked off the pillowcase that was still damp from my tears, and started filling it with things I needed. I put in all the food I thought I could carry, and on impulse, I put in a kitchen knife in case I needed protection. Living in the city had made me wary. I wrote a note to Flint and stuck it on the door as I left. I told him that I had gone back home and that he should bring the rest of my things and some food.

I walked as fast as I could for the first hour, anxious to arrive home by dark and afraid that if I stopped to rest I might lose my nerve and turn back.

During the second hour, I walked more slowly. By the fifth hour my feet were dragging, and the pillowcase felt like it had a ton of rocks in it. I'd gotten so overheated that I had taken off my coat and stuffed it inside the pillowcase. Now I was cooler, but my pack was heavier. My hands cramped from carrying it so many hours.

It had taken eight hours to walk home, but now I was within a few minutes of being there. For the past hour I had been walking through the forest I knew and loved. Each tree was a familiar old friend; each rock a marker along the trail. No, I could never get lost here; not like in the city with all of its look-alike streets and tall buildings that blocked out the sun.

I reached the crest of the hill and looked down toward the valley to see our house.

The house was gone! There was nothing left.

It was gone! The house was gone! There was nothing left but a few scattered logs, charred black from a fire.

Forgetting how tired I was, I ran down the hill with my bag bouncing against my back.

I stopped where the front door should have been and looked at the twisted rubble in front of me. There was nothing left. It couldn't have taken long for this old shack to burn to the ground.

I kicked through the ashes. It had been burned down months ago, probably right after Cloud and I left the valley.

I knew it wasn't an accident. Someone, either one of my uncles or one of Grandmother's Navajo friends had set a torch to the house, thinking that since she had died inside, her spirit could be trapped in the house and unable to find its way to the next life.

I slumped down in the ashes. I had come home, but there was no longer a home.

It was getting dark. I didn't want to spend the night out in the open. If I hurried, I could make it to Cloud's cabin before nightfall. At least I would have some shelter. I forced myself to my feet and threw my bag back over my shoulder, staggering under the weight.

I avoided looking in the direction of the barn and kept my eyes focused on the path in front of my feet.

"I shouldn't have come back," I told myself. "It was stupid. There is nothing here anymore. Everything is gone; the people, the animals, the house. All are gone now. Only I am here, wandering around like a lost spirit haunting the valley.

I reached Cloud's cabin just as the sun sank out of sight.

I took a candle and some matches out of my bag. I lit the candle. It didn't give much light, but it was better than this awful darkness.

I sat down on the floor, opened a can of beans, and leaned against the wall while I ate them.

The trader hadn't left anything behind when he bought Cloud out. There was nothing but an empty room. Not one stick of wood or scrap of paper remained.

I was exhausted now and couldn't keep my eyes open any longer. I reached into my bag one more time and pulled out the knife. I rolled my coat into a pillow, blew out the candle, and lay down on the floor, still holding the knife tightly in my hand and wishing I hadn't tried to come home.

I woke up stiff and cold in the early morning. There was a faint hint of frost on the ground, and patches of fog were hanging low in the valley waiting to disappear as the sun climbed higher.

I ate a can of cold chili for breakfast and put my things back into my bag. After a last look around, I headed back to town.

As I walked, I tried not to think about the pile of ashes that used to be my home. I tried not to think about anything except putting one foot in front of the other.

My feet were aching when I walked up to the door of my apartment, eight hours later. My note was still on the door. Flint hadn't been here. As I pulled the note off the door and wrinkled it up in my hand, I was glad Flint wouldn't know about my plans to go back home. I didn't want him to know what a fool I'd made out of myself.

What was I going to do now? I couldn't go back home; it was gone. I didn't belong in the city.

Why had the wind called me back to the reservation when he must have known there was nothing left to go back to? Was he playing a joke on me? Yes, that must be it. The old Indian gods often played cruel jokes on people, and he had played a joke on me. He must be angry at me about something. I was doing something wrong, and he had punished me. What had I done, what? Then it came to me. The wind didn't like me going to church. That had to be it. I would have to stop going to church or he would do something terrible to me. This had only been a warning.

I took my things out of the pillowcase. It was filthy from the dust along the road where I had dragged it behind me the last mile, too weary to carry it any longer.

I sank into a steaming, hot bath and let it soak the aches out of my tired body. I was thankful for the luxury of a hot bath. City life had spoiled me. I would have missed the hot running water and the electricity and the refrigerator and stove. City life was making me soft and lazy.

The next few days were empty and long. When it was dark, I went to bed. I said, "At last, another day is over." I dreaded the next dawn. I hated to wake up in the mornings. I pulled a chair up in front of the window and sat in it for hours, watching

128

people walking past or cars going down the street or sometimes I just stared into space not seing anything at all.

I don't remember when I first noticed it, but I caught myself watching a flashing sign about two blocks away. "LIQUOR." "LIQUOR." It flashed many times a minute. Pretty soon I was watching it more than I was watching anything else.

Then I remembered that Flint had left a half-full bottle of whiskey in the kitchen cupboard the last time he was here. The more I thought about it, the more I was tempted to drink it. I didn't really like to drink. The liquor tasted bad and made my head ache, but Flint drank a lot and so did my other uncles, so there must be something to it. Maybe I just hadn't drunk enough. Maybe it took a lot to make you feel good.

I left my chair by the window, went to the cupboard, and took out the bottle of whiskey. I held it in my hands and looked at the pale brown color. When I opened it, the fumes made my eyes water. I almost put the cap back on, but I decided I might as well go ahead and drink it. After all, I had nothing to lose. Maybe it would pass the time and make me feel better.

I poured a small amount into a glass. It took me several minutes to finally choke it down. It tasted bad and burned my throat, but I kept at it. The next drink went down faster, and I was feeling warm and sleepy. *I must be on the right track now,* I thought. I poured another drink.

The room started to reel, and the light hurt my eyes, so I crawled into my bed and turned off the lamp. In seconds I was asleep. I didn't wake up until late the next day.

I felt awful when I woke up and decided to drink a little more whiskey to make my head stop spinning. I passed the day by taking a drink, taking a nap, taking another drink.

Somewhere between the drinks and the naps, depression started creeping up on me. Questions echoed in my head, *Why keep trying? Why not give up?*

I don't remember leaving the apartment, but I found myself standing on the edge of the curb of the street. In the foggy haze of my mind, I kept thinking *Pick a fast car and step in front of it and it will all be over.* Then I saw a car coming much faster than the others. I closed my eyes tightly, took a big breath, and stepped off the curb!

There was the screeching of brakes and the squealing of tires as I waited for the car to hit me.

It was taking too long! I should have already been run down. I opened my eyes in time to see the car swerve around me. As it passed, the driver shook his fist at me and yelled, "Stupid, drunken Indian—" the rest of his words were drowned out by his car motor as he sped down the street.

I was suddenly very sober and standing in the middle of a very busy street. Horns seemed to be honking all around me as I made a mad dash for the curb.

With very weak legs I walked back to the apartment. I would have to find some other way to kill myself. I finished the rest of the whiskey and threw myself across the bed. I tried to think of a quick, easy way to die. I didn't have a gun or any sleeping pills. I had heard of people drinking themselves to death, but that could take years. I didn't want to be around that long. I was in a hurry to get it over with.

All the next day I tried to think of a way to end my life. I thought of dozens of ways to die, but I came to the conclusion that there is no easy way to die. Dying is hard.

I also came to the conclusion I was too poor to die. I was too broke to buy a gun or sleeping pills. I lived on the ground floor, so I couldn't jump out a window. I didn't own a piece of string, let alone a rope, so I couldn't hang myself. Indians have very little body hair, so I didn't even own razor blades. The stove in the apartment was electric, so I couldn't use gas to kill myself. The only way I could afford to die was to jump in front of a car, and I had lost my nerve. I couldn't go through that again! I was too poor to die. I would have to get a job and save some money to buy something to use to kill myself! It was so funny I had to laugh about it. Living was hard, but dying was harder.

Chapter Ten

The next day I visited Reverend McPherson.

"Do you have a job yet?" he asked.

"No." I didn't tell him that I wasn't even looking.

"I was just thinking I could use some help here in the office. It would only be for a couple of days and I couldn't pay you much," he said.

"What kind of work?" I asked.

"Well, for one thing, all the books in the church library need to be listed. Some need repairs and new labels. I need some missionary letters sorted and filed. Things like that."

I thought for a moment and then said, "Thanks anyway, but I don't think he would like it."

"Who wouldn't like it? Your uncle?"

"The wind. The wind wouldn't like me working in another god's house."

"There is only one God," he said.

"But if the wind isn't god, then who is the wind? Or what is the wind?" I asked.

"That's hard to say. I guess scientists could give you some sort of answer about high and low pressures and cold fronts and such things, but I know that's not what you're looking for." Then his eyes lit up, and he smiled. "I don't mean to be frivolous, but I just remembered a poem I knew as a child. It was written by Robert Louis Stevenson. He apparently had his own questions about who or what the wind was—let's see if I can remember it, it's been many a year since I was a child—"

I saw you toss the kites on high
And blow the birds about the sky;
And all around I heard you pass,
Like ladies' skirts across the grass—
O wind, a-blowing all day long,
O wind, that sings so loud a song!

I saw the different things you did,
But always you yourself you hid.
I felt you push, I heard you call,
I could not see yourself at all—
O wind, a-blowing all day long,
O wind, that sings so loud a song!

O you that are so strong and cold,
O blower, are you young or old?
Are you a beast of field and tree,
Or just a stronger child than me?
O wind, a-blowing all day long,
O wind, that sings so loud a song!

"What was that last part again?" I asked as soon as he had finished.

He repeated it slowly so it could sink in.

"Was this man an Indian?" I asked.

"No, he was an Englishman. He wrote the poem over a hundred years ago."

"He should have been an Indian. He understood the wind." I repeated the lines I could remember, "I felt you push, I heard you call . . . O you that are strong and cold, O blower, are you young or old? Are you a beast of field and tree, or just a stronger child than me?" I nodded. "I like that. Do you know any more poems about the wind?"

I twisted my fingers together and chewed on my lip. "What is your God really like?"

"He is everything to everyone. The Bible says, 'As a father pities his children so the Lord pities those who fear him.' "

133

"My father abandoned me," I said. "I don't like to think about God being like a father."

"It also says, 'As one whom his mother comforts, so I will comfort you,'" he quoted.

"My mother ran off and left me years ago. I've never heard from her since," I reminded him.

"He is a friend who sticks closer than a brother," he said.

"I've never had any friends, and I don't have any brothers or sisters," I challenged him.

He shrugged and smiled, "Well, it also says, 'Husbands love your wives as Christ loved His Church,' but since you are not married, that won't mean much to you, will it?"

"No. I guess none of that applies to me," I said.

"Maybe none of these verses, but somewhere in the Bible there is one verse that will be special to you, and when you hear it, it will unlock your heart and your mind to the spiritual truths of the Bible. Then it will all fall into place for you. Once you hear that verse your life will be changed. You will never be the same again. We will keep searching until we find that special verse that was written there for Crying Wind." His hand fell gently on his Bible.

"I don't believe there is a verse in there for me."

"There is a verse in here for everyone. The Bible speaks to every heart."

"It doesn't mention the wind," I said. Certainly I was right this time.

"It mentions the wind many times."

I leaned forward. "What does it say?"

"I can't remember all of them, but I could look up every time it's mentioned in the Bible and make a list. Then you look up the verses when you have time."

"All right. I guess it wouldn't hurt to know what your book had to say about the wind." I shrugged casually, but I was in-

I began hunting through the Bible for every mention of the wind.

terested. When he made out the list, I folded it carefully and put it into my pocket.

Later that night, after I had gone to bed, I propped myself up with some pillows and began hunting through the Bible for every mention of the wind. *After all,* I thought, *it isn't as if I were studying about this God. I was just trying to learn more about the wind.*

It took a long time to find all the verses, because I didn't know the order of the books of the Bible, but I finally had all the verses looked up and written down.

The first mention of the wind was in Genesis 8:1, "And God remembered Noah, and every living thing, and all the cattle that was with him in the ark: and God made a wind to pass over the earth, and the waters asswaged."

In Exodus 15:10 it read, "Thou didst blow with thy wind."

Job spoke of the wind twice: "my life is wind" (Job 7:7), and "the words of thy mouth be like a strong wind" (Job 8:2).

Over and over I read the verses about the wind, and there were a few that seemed to reach out to me.

"Who hath ascended up into heaven, or descended? Who hath gathered the wind in his fists?" (Proverbs 30:4).

"Lo, he that formeth the mountains and createth the wind . . . The LORD, The God of Hosts, is his name" (Amos 4:13).

It spoke of the Lord sending out a great wind into the sea, but when I read Matthew 8:26 where it said Jesus "arose and rebuked the winds," I knew I'd found something!

Why had the wind allowed this other God to rebuke him and to order him to be still? You didn't give orders to someone unless he was under you and you didn't follow orders unless the person giving them was stronger or wiser or had authority and power. I was becoming curious about this new God. Was it possible that He really could have created the wind?

It was beginning to seem that the only time I was even halfway happy was when I was at the church talking to Reverend McPherson or Audrey. I told myself it was only boredom and loneliness that drove me back there time after time. After all, they were the only people I knew except Flint, and he seldom had time for me. I was beginning to show up on the doorstep of the church more and more often. I liked sitting in Reverend McPherson's comfortable office with its shelves of books and the cluttered desk and flowering plants beside the windows.

"How are you today?" he greeted me.

"I don't know," I said truthfully.

He smiled knowingly. "You would be surprised how many people feel exactly the same way you do. They know something is bothering them, but they don't know what it is. Maybe if you talked about how you feel—maybe I could help?"

I sat in silence for several minutes. "It's no use, I can't find the right words. When my heart is full, my head is empty. When I am alone I can think of many things to say. All the way here as I walk along, I practice what I will say when I see you. Then when I come through the door, my words stay outside and the wind blows them away." I swallowed hard. "I am just wasting your time."

"No, you aren't wasting my time. Sometimes it's good to be with someone even if you don't say a single word. Sometimes you can learn more about a person by his silences than by his words." He paused. "Do you think it would help you to write your thoughts and questions down? You could carry a little notebook, and when you thought of a question or had an idea you wanted to discuss, you could write it down. If you felt like sharing it with me, I could read the notebook when you came back."

He began rummaging through the clutter of his desk. "Ah! Here it is! I'll even get you started with this little notebook. I bought it the other day. I hadn't had time to use it yet so it's new, for some new ideas from Crying Wind." He smiled and leaned across the desk and handed it to me. He reached into his shirt pocket and pulled out a pen. "Now you have the notebook, and you have the pen. I know you have the ideas. All you have to do is get the three of them together."

I reached out eagerly and took the gifts he offered and smiled as I fanned through the notebook and saw the clean, fresh pages waiting to be filled.

"I think I'll go now." I stood up. "I want to go home and write something."

"I'll be looking forward to reading it." He walked me to the door.

"Maybe I'll see you sometime," I said.

"I hope so."

I was reluctant to leave. "Maybe Friday," I added.

"Anytime you feel like coming, you are welcome."

We shook hands, and I walked down the church steps. When I reached the bottom step, I turned and looked back. He was standing just inside the door, watching me.

I waved with my hand that held the notebook and pen and hurried down the street. When I was almost half-way home, I was so eager to get home, I ran the rest of the way. I was completely out of breath by the time I reached the apartment. I yanked off my coat and sat down at the table and opened the notebook. I took the pen in my hand and wrote "Crying Wind" in bold letters across the first page.

I paused only a second, and then it seemed as if the pen was magic. Words and ideas poured from me. I wrote several pages before I stopped to read what I had written. Writing was so simple, such an easy thing to do. You could write anything that was in your heart or on your mind. Why did speaking have to always be such a hard, painful thing to do?

I wrote some questions that I wanted to ask Reverend Mc-

There seemed to be thousands of unused words in my heart, waiting to be set free.

Pherson about this man Jesus and His Father, God. I remembered that Reverend McPherson had asked me who I thought the wind was, so I began to describe the wind on the paper. Then I wrote about the Spirit Horse. There seemed to be thousands of unused words in my heart, waiting to be set free. I couldn't write fast enough to keep up with my thoughts.

I wrote until the last page was filled. I put the pen down and looked at the clock. It was two o'clock in the morning. I noticed how stiff my fingers were from holding the pen all these hours, and I stretched my muscles that were tired from bending over the notebook so long. I felt good. Thoughts and feelings that had been buried in silence for years had finally fought their way to the surface. I smiled as I fell asleep, and I knew that I couldn't wait until Friday to see Reverend McPherson. I would see him tomorrow.

As soon as I saw him, I handed him the poems I had written. I waited anxiously while he read them. It was important to me that he like them.

THE WIND

by CRYING WIND

The Summer wind is warm, passionate, and alive. She caresses the flowers until they tremble with emotion. The trees whisper the mysteries of the forest, and the wild roses blush at the secrets told. A swing moves gently to and fro as if the ghost of a small girl of ages past still laughs and plays beneath the same tree.

Time has slipped away now. The wind is older, wiser, perhaps a little crisp and angry because it cannot fight its fate.

It carelessly tosses around the dried leaves of autumn in the same way a jilted lover might toss aside his dreams. The brown grass scratches against the broken stems of flowers whose faded blossoms have long since been blown away.

Now Winter is here. The wind is old and bitter and as cold and lonely as a widow. The leaves are covered with snow, and the moon is brittle and bright as it gazes at its beauty in the ice on the pond.

The swing is now still, weighted down by snow that holds it prisoner in silent bondage.

It blows again, but the spirit and strength are gone. The wrinkled old woman screams around the houses, begging to be let inside so she might warm her chilled body by the fire. She rattles the windows and bangs at the doors, but none will answer her, and she is left alone in the night. In anger she tugs at the swing and releases it from its slavery.

Then the old woman wind moves slowly down the valley and disappears into the night. She goes without a sound; silently, mournfully. The trees make no move to wave goodbye. They only stand, watching, perhaps a little sad, perhaps with no feeling at all.

ALONE

(Written for Pascal)

It's too late, but now we'll mourn;
Some will speak of him with scorn.
Perhaps if once someone had said,
"I love you," he would not be dead.

Time is not marked by days, months, or years,
It's marked by emptiness and tears.
Was he really so very bad?
Or was he only lonely and sad?
He lived alone and died that way, too.
No one cared, not even a few.
No one will know the reason why,
He shut out life and preferred to die.
People passed him by on the street,
He wasn't important, no need to speak.
Killed himself, that's what they said.
If some had loved him,
        He wouldn't be dead.

SPIRIT HORSE

by CRYING WIND

There will be no sleep for me tonight,
The wind is crying and the moon is bright.
It's only then that you come to me,
When the moon is silver and the wind is free.

Wild-eyed and prancing, you stand on the lawn,
To carry me away and return before dawn.
The raging wind is your fiery breath,
Your hooves make thunder as we race with death!

You carry me to the edge of the sea,
The fierce, pounding waves crash around me.
I feel the salt spray against my face,
Then you gallop away at your deadly pace!

Up through the foothills and valley we go,
And stand on top of mountains with the whole world below.
Then across the desert through the dust and sands,
Onward we roam to strange, distant lands.

Your hooves keep pounding, and I feel your power,
You quicken your pace at the midnight hour.
With your neck outstretched and you mane flowing white,
We gallop on through the stormy night!

141

Wild-eyed and prancing, you stand there on the lawn.

My heart grows heavy as you turn around,
And we head back over familiar ground.
I know that soon there will be an Eastern light,
And our ride will be over until tomorrow night.

Spirit Horse, come back to me. Don't leave me here alone.
I won't fear death if I ride with you, into the great unknown.
Wild-eyed and prancing, you stand on the lawn,
To carry me away and return before dawn.

He finished reading them and he smiled when he looked up at me.

"They are good. They are really good and I like them. In fact, "Spirit Horse" is beautiful. I could tell there was a lot of you in it. I think we are finally finding out the secret of Crying Wind." He handed the notebook back to me. "You should try to get these published."

"No one would want to read anything Crying Wind wrote," I said.

He leaned back in his chair. His eyes met mine and held them.

"Who is Crying Wind?" he asked. I could tell by his voice he was expecting an answer.

"I'm nobody," I said. I thought I was finished, but his eyes still held mine as he waited for more of an answer.

"I'm the accidental offspring of two people who hated each other. I never saw my father's face because he abandoned my mother before I was born, and she hated him for it. My mother was young and didn't want to be tied down with a baby she hadn't wanted in the first place, so she left me with my grandmother on the reservation. It didn't matter anyway. I didn't need parents. Grandmother took care of me, and my uncles were around. We did all right." My jaws seemed to tighten as I spoke. "I'm a worthless half-breed; two people trying to live in one body." I added bitterly, "That's who Crying Wind is—nobody."

143

His fingertips touched lightly together, and he spoke softly. "Then I know more about Crying Wind than you do. You paint pictures—that makes you an artist. You write beautiful poetry—that makes you a poet. You are a lovely young girl with a keen mind who could have an unlimited future. Your parents did not create you—God created you! The same God who created the heavens and the earth created you. You are not what your parents made you. You can be whatever you want to be. You have a special worth; you are unique. There is not another person in the world exactly like Crying Wind. God made you and you are valuable to Him. You are worth more to Him than a star, because He has millions of stars, but He has only one of you! You are worth more to Him than the mountains or the rivers."

It was more than I could understand. "Worth more than a star shining in the sky at night?" I asked.

"Yes!" he said. "Worth more than the very life of His own Son. In the Bible it says, 'For God so loved Crying Wind that He allowed His only Son to die in her place so that she could have eternal life!'"

"It doesn't say that," I argued, knowing my name was not in the Bible.

"It could say that because you are so valuable to God, that if you were the only person in the whole world, Jesus would still go to die on the cross for you. Never say you are nobody, because you are somebody special. You are special to God and to Audrey and me. I have the feeling that someday thousands of people are going to hear from Crying Wind. I don't know God's plan for your life, but I do know this; He has a special plan for you. Maybe He'll use your artwork or your poetry or some other talent that is buried now but will come to light later. God has His hand on you, and when you stop fighting Him and let Him guide you, great things will happen!" He paused. "Would you like me to pray for you?"

144

"No," I answered quickly. "I don't want to believe in your god."

He smiled. "I think you believe in Him already, or you wouldn't be so afraid that He would answer my prayers that you would become a Christian."

I studied him closely. He really believed every word he was saying. He thought I was worth something. Was I really worth more to God than a star? On the way home that night, I watched the stars and thought, *maybe—maybe I really am worth something after all!*

Chapter Eleven

Flint was waiting for me when I got home.

"Where have you been?" he asked.

Without thinking I answered, "I went down to a church and talked to the minister—" I stopped. I knew I had been wrong to tell him.

"You've been in a church!" he exploded.

"Yes." I admitted but added quickly, "But I didn't go to a real church meeting. I was only talking with the minister." It was too late to undo the damage.

"You must be loco! Why did you do that? You are an Indian. You don't need any Long Robes!"

Flint was using the Indian term for missionaries. The first missionaries to our people had been Catholic priests who had worn long robes. Ever since then, any white religious leader was called Long Robe.

Flint's voice was hard. His eyes were full of hate.

"The Kickapoo have never accepted the white man's religion. More Kickapoo have hung onto the old ways than any other tribe. We are proud that the white man has never taught his religion to us or taught our children in our schools. We've always burned down his schools, and in the old days, we burned down his churches, too. We killed the Long Robes who came into our land! Why were you talking to a Long Robe?"

"I don't know," I said weakly. "I just don't know anyone else here. We just talked about poems and things."

I'd never seen Flint so angry before. His jaw was set so tight that the muscles in his neck stood out and his hands were clenched into fists.

"Now you listen and hear my words!" he said between tightly clenched teeth, "I never wanted to take care of you in the first place, but Cloud dumped you in my lap. I am stuck with you. I promised to keep an eye on you because you are family. Up until now you haven't been much trouble, but I'm warning you—no niece of mine is going to get mixed up with those snake-in-the-grass white people or that crazy religion of theirs! Don't you ever go back there again, or I'll skin you alive!" With those words hanging in the air, he stomped out and slammed the door behind him.

At first I decided to obey Flint. After all, he was my uncle. I would stay away from church. After a few days passed I realized how much I missed my visits with the McPhersons. Up until now I thought I could take it or leave it, but without Reverend McPherson's friendship and Audrey's warmth, there was a big, empty hole in my life. I missed church and wanted to return, but I was afraid to go against Flint.

Late in the afternon the phone rang, and I jumped at the loud noise. I had never had a phone call before.

"Hello?"

"Is this Crying Wind?"

"Yes."

"This is Audrey. We've missed you dear. Are you all right?"

"Yes."

"We were hoping you might come to the church tonight. There is a special service for Christmas. We really would love to have you with us."

"OK," I said and hung up. After I hung up, I wondered if she had finished talking, or if I just cut her off. I would never get used to speaking into a machine and talking to voices without faces. You should see a person when you speak to him, not talk into a machine.

If the church had seemed beautiful to me before, now it was overwhelming. Candles seemed to be burning everywhere. Pine boughs and poinsettias decorated the altar and the area around the altar. The altar itself had a manger scene.

I walked up to the altar to get a closer look. Snow fell off my coat and dropped on the carpet, leaving a little trail behind me.

On the altar was a small stable with donkeys and cattle and sheep. In one corner was a man and a young woman who were bending over a newborn baby lying in a manger. The flickering

I realized that these tiny figures represented real people.

candles made them look alive. I had heard the story of the Nativity before, but it had never seemed like anything except a church legend. Now, as I stood here looking at these tiny figures, I suddenly knew they represented real people. Mary and Joseph had been real people, and if that was true, then the baby Jesus had really been born. The wise men and the shepherds had believed it and had come to see the Christ Child. It wasn't just a pretty story any longer. It was true!

I slowly reached out my hand. I wanted to touch the baby in the manger, but just as my fingers were about to feel it, I heard the door open and people coming in. I went back to the benches and sat down. A moment later a woman sat down beside me. She leaned over and whispered, "We are so happy to have you here tonight. My name is Sally."

"Sally?" I repeated. White people had strange names. They were only sounds instead of words. It was easy to remember a name like Song Bird or Gray Fox, but a name like Sally gave no pictures to the mind.

She smiled, "Do you care if I sit with you? I don't like to sit alone. It is so much nicer to sit with a friend."

When she said the word *friend,* our eyes met, and I knew she meant me. She smiled again, and I knew now that I would never forget her name, Sally.

The service was starting. Reverend McPherson stepped behind his pulpit, opened his Bible, and read the story of the birth of Christ. The choir sang songs more beautiful than anything I had ever heard; "O Holy Night," "What Child Is This," and others.

I stole glances at some of the people as they sang. It was plain from their faces that they believed every word they sang. At the end of the singing, Sally closed the hymnbook and said, "I love Christmas carols. I wish we used them more than once a year."

"But why do you use your best songs only once a year?" I

asked. "I would sing these songs all year. They sound good."

"Yes, they do sound good, don't they?" she agreed.

The service was over, and everyone left for home too quickly.

I still felt a warm peace from the service as I walked home. Fresh snow was falling and looked like sparkling little stars. My footprints were the only ones in sight. I felt as if I were the only person who lived in this clean, white world of snow.

As I turned toward home, I saw that there were fresh tire tracks leading up to my apartment. The snow had been cleaned off my doorstep, and there was something on it.

It was a large cardboard box with my name written on it.

I unlocked my door, flipped on the light, and hauled the box inside. It was heavy and hard to move.

I shut the door, took off my coat, dropped to my knees beside the box, and carefully opened the lid.

Inside the box were a dozen cans of soup, vegetables, and fruit, and a small canned ham. There were also two packages wrapped in bright red paper. I picked up the largest package and tore the paper off. It was the most beautiful red sweater I had ever seen. I touched it to my cheek. How could anything feel so soft? I put it on and buttoned it; it fit perfectly. I reached for the next package and opened it. It was a book about Christian Indians. As I opened the cover, an envelope fell out and landed in my lap. I put the book down and opened the envelope. It was a Christmas card; a beautiful card with the manger scene on it. Inside was ten dollars, and the card was signed, "Merry Christmas from your friends at church."

I held the card in trembling fingers. All this? All this for me? No, it couldn't be. It was a mistake. I checked the box again. That was my name on it, but why? Why would the people at church want to give me anything for Christmas? I was a stranger to them—but the card had been signed "friends." Were they

It was the most beautiful red sweater I had ever seen.

really my friends? Why would they do it? I had nothing anyone could want.

I sat on the floor, still wearing my new red sweater, and took
each can of food out of the box and looked at it, knowing how
good the food would taste. I looked at the book again and put
the ten dollars back inside the cover.

I propped the Christmas card up against the lamp beside my
bed. The manger scene, Mary, Joseph, and Baby Jesus, was just
like on the altar at church.

I carefully folded my sweater and put it away, touching it one
last time before I closed the drawer. Then I put the canned

goods away, stacking them on the shelf in neat little rows. So much, and all for me!

Early the next morning there was a knock on my door. It was Flint.

"Hi," he said. "I just thought I'd drop by to see how you are doing."

"I'm so happy to see you! What have you been doing? I haven't seen you for a while. Will you stay and have lunch with me?"

He ignored my questions, but I put some food in the oven to cook. He wouldn't pass up a hot meal. He was silent for a while, and then he said, "I quit my job. Never liked it much anyway, so I decided to quit."

"What will you do now?" I suddenly found myself sounding like Reverend McPherson did when I told him I had quit my job.

"Oh, I don't know. I'll find something. One job is as good as the next. I can always get a job wrangling horses on the Circle L Ranch. It's only ten miles from here." He paced the floor, stopped, and tapped the cardboard box with his toe.

"What's the box for?"

"Some people gave me a box of things for Christmas." I said. I wanted to tell him who it was from and how wonderful it had made me feel, but I knew I didn't dare. I was glad he dropped the subject.

As we ate, we talked about people we knew and about our family. I asked him if he had heard from Cloud. He said he hadn't and didn't expect ever to hear from him again. That made me feel sad because I missed Cloud. I still hoped he would come back someday.

After he had finished eating, he leaned back in his chair and patted his stomach. According to Indian custom, he belched loudly to show his appreciation.

"That was mighty good Cry. You're not a bad cook. Too bad you can't get a husband to cook for, but you're too skinny to be worth much."

"I'm worth more than a star," I said.

"What are you talking about?" he asked.

"Oh, nothing. Can you spend the day with me?" I asked.

"No, I have to go now. Thanks for the grub." He stepped out the door, and the wind blew snow inside.

"Please come back soon Flint. Don't stay away so long this time."

"Sure. I'll see you sometime," he said and headed for his truck.

I waved good-bye, knowing "see you sometime" could mean a couple of days, a couple of weeks, or even several months. I wished he would spend the day with me. It would have been nice to have someone to talk to.

I sank into a soft chair and reached for the book from the church. Soon I was deep in the story.

A few nights later I walked to the church to thank Reverend McPherson for the Christmas gifts. We only talked a few minutes when he said, "Well, it's nearly time for the service to start. I'd better get the lights turned on in the sanctuary. You would be more than welcome to join us."

"What are you going to do?" I asked.

"Tonight is a healing service. We pray for those who are ill, hurt, or in trouble."

"I'm not sick. I don't need healed," I said as I put on my coat.

"I think there is a little child in you who needs healing from many hurts in the past. I think that little child was hurt so many times by so many people that you have locked her away behind a stone wall so she wouldn't get hurt anymore. Don't you want to let her out?"

I didn't answer.

He went on quickly. "There will only be a handful of people here tonight. They are all very nice people, good Christians. They would like to help you if they could. You could just sit quietly in the back if you wanted. You wouldn't have to do anything or say anything."

I almost said yes. I wanted to stay, but for some reason that I didn't understand, I just shook my head. I could see he was disappointed. After I got outside and stood on the front steps of the church a few minutes, I almost talked myself into going back inside, but then I heard singing in the sanctuary. The service had already started. I had waited too long to make up my mind. I walked home feeling like I had missed out on something.

Chapter Twelve

I thought about it all week and decided that next Wednesday night I would go to the church. I would stay and sit in the back and listen to what the people said and watch what they did. If I sat in the back, I could always leave anytime I wanted.

When Wednesday night finally came around, I was just getting ready to leave for the church when Flint drove up. It was the first time I hadn't wanted to see him. I knew if I invited him inside I wouldn't get to church, so I met him on the steps and shut the door behind me.

"Hi. You leaving?" he asked as he climbed out of his pickup.

"Yes, I didn't know you were coming tonight, and I already have plans."

"Date?" he asked.

"No." I couldn't tell him I was going to church.

"Can I drive you someplace?" he offered.

"No. I want to walk. Thanks anyway. Maybe you could come over tomorrow night and eat with me. I'll make some fry bread for you." I knew how he loved fry bread. I was hoping he would start thinking about tomorrow evening and forget about tonight.

"OK." He got back into his truck. "Sure I can't drop you off someplace?"

I shook my head, and he left. I was glad to see him turn down the street and go the opposite direction of the church.

I hurried along, not paying any attention to anything around me. If I had been watching I would have noticed a truck following about a block behind me.

It wasn't until I cut across the parking lot next to the church that I heard someone driving behind me.

My heart sank when I turned and saw Flint. He had followed me to see where I was going.

"Hi," I said. I wished he didn't look so angry.

"Is this the big secret?" he nodded toward the church. "This is why you aren't home half the time. You've been coming to this place."

"But it's a good place, Flint!" I argued.

"How can it be a good place when it turns you against your family and against your own people and your own gods?" he said sharply.

"I'm not turning against anyone. I'm the same person I've always been."

"No, you're not! You're different, and I don't like the change. The rest of the family isn't going to like it either! Whatever lies they've been teaching you in there, you had better forget them and remember who you are! That religion is for the white man; let him keep it. You stay where you belong and stop trying to be someone you aren't."

"Why are you so angry? What difference does it make if I come here? I'm not a believer, I just come because the people are nice and I like to hear the stories and the music. It's better than sitting at home all the time."

"You can come with me if you're lonely."

"You never go anyplace except bars and peyote ceremonies," I said. I regretted it as soon as I saw the look in his eyes.

"Peyote is the father god of your own people!" He was angrier than I had ever seen him. "These people are poisoning your mind. Now get in the truck and come with me. Don't you ever come back here again!"

He reached out and grabbed my arm and started pulling me toward his truck.

The whip sliced my back.

I yanked free and started toward the church.

"You come here!" he shouted after me, but I kept walking. I heard a door on the truck open and thought he was leaving, but before I had taken three more steps he was beside me.

"I'm warning you, Crying Wind, if you don't come with me now you'll be sorry!" He shook his leather horse whip in my face.

I'd seen him use it on horses before, but I knew he would never use it on me. It was just a threat.

"Leave me alone," I said and started to turn away. Flint cracked the whip. It came down hard across my left shoulder and my arm. I staggered backward under the blow. When I saw him raising the whip again I turned my back and hunched my shoulders and waited for the next stinging blow. The whip sliced across my back. I felt a chill go through my body like ice was being rubbed across my skin. After a couple more blows, the whip didn't hurt anymore. The shock of it made my body numb. I felt as if I were somewhere outside my body, and Flint was beating someone else. I don't know how many more times he hit me. He finally stopped.

I waited for another blow. When there wasn't one, I straightened up and faced him.

Flint stood there with his arms hanging limp at his sides. The whip looked as if it were about to fall out of his half-open hand. He shook his head a few times and stepped backwards.

"Don't go there anymore," he said in a hoarse voice, but there was no power in his threat. He seemed like a shell standing there. This man wasn't the uncle I had known. This man in front of me looked thin and tired. His eyes looked like the eyes of a hunted animal who was too tired to run anymore and just waited for death.

I hadn't uttered a sound. My throat was too dry to speak.

Flint turned and walked away. In a few seconds I heard the motor of his truck as he drove away.

I walked around the corner of the church and climbed up the steps. The numbness had gone, and my back felt like it was on fire. Every move I made sent fresh flames of pain across my shoulders. It took all my strength to pull open the heavy door and ease inside. The lights seemed too bright and the floor seemed to be moving. Reverend McPherson was coming toward me. My legs turned to water, and I sank to the floor. The floor felt cool against my face. I closed my eyes and let the spinning darkness catch me.

"I think she is waking up." A voice from far away spoke quietly.

I tried to open my eyes.

A cool hand touched my forehead. "How do you feel?" asked the voice.

I finally got my eyes open long enough to see Audrey standing over me.

I was lying, on my stomach, on a soft bed. I started to move. The fire started burning my back again, so I laid still.

"Your back is hurt pretty bad. I put some medicine on it and

158

"Your back is hurt pretty bad."

some bandages. You probably should see a doctor," she said.
I could feel her gentle fingers rubbing something cool across my
back.

"No." My voice was weak. "No doctor."

"What happened? We can help you. No matter what it is,
we can help." She finished wiping my back and took the bloody
pieces of cotton and dropped them into the wastebasket. "If you
are up to it, my husband wants to talk to you."

"I'm all right," I said. She helped me sit up on the bed. She
went to the closet and took out a blouse and helped me slip into
it.

"This will be too big for you, but yours is—is torn," she said,
and her voice cracked. After she had helped me put on the fresh

159

blouse, she picked up my torn, bloody one and dropped it into the wastebasket on her way out of the room.

I sat on the edge of the bed and held onto the bedpost to keep from shaking.

There was a knock on the door and I heard Reverend McPherson ask, "May I come in?"

"Yes."

"My wife is making some hot tea for you. She'll bring it in in a minute. How are you feeling?"

I started to shrug my shoulders and pain shot across my back and the look on my face showed exactly how I felt.

"Can you tell me what happened?"

"My uncle—" I took a deep breath, "My uncle and I got into a fight— he won." I would have smiled but I couldn't manage it.

"I don't understand," he said.

"My uncle has been warning me not to come here. Tonight he was waiting outside the church. He tried to make me leave with him. I wouldn't go, so he beat me."

"Do you mean to say that your own uncle beat you for coming here?"

I nodded.

"I don't believe it! While I was sitting inside the church praying for tonight's service, you were being beaten less than a hundred feet from my door! Things like this just can't happen. Not in America. Not in this day and age! He can't do that to you! We'll call the police and have him arrested!"

"I can't do that," I said.

"Of course you can! No one can treat you like that and get away with it!"

"He's my uncle; I can't have him arrested. If I did that— well, it's just a family feud. Things like this happen all the time back on the reservation—"

"You're not on the reservation now," he argued. "You deserve protection. You have a right to go to church." He acted like he wanted to say more but was too angry to find the words.

"It doesn't matter. It didn't really hurt that much," I said lamely, knowing it had hurt more than anything I had ever known. Maybe it wasn't the sting of the whip that hurt as much as knowing Flint had held the whip.

He took a deep breath. "I've never been so angry."

Just then Audrey came with a cup of hot tea. The two of them sat in silence while I drank it. When I was finished, I handed her the cup.

"I'd better go now," I said.

"No," they both said together. Then Audrey said, "We can't let you leave in your condition. You're hurt, and you shouldn't be alone. You'll stay here with us until you're better. Besides, I don't think it is safe for you to return to your apartment tonight. What if your uncle showed up?"

"Don't worry about me," I said.

"We have to worry about you because we love you," Audrey said.

Her answer took my breath away. Never in my life had I heard those words spoken to me. "We love you," she had said.

She went to her dresser and pulled out a nightgown. "You'll stay with us," she said firmly. "In the morning I can go to your apartment and get some of your things. You can stay as long as you like, and we won't let anything happen to you."

I didn't argue. It was possible that Flint might be back home waiting for me, and I really did want to stay here where I was safe. Safe—such a nice word.

Reverend McPherson left. Audrey helped me get ready for bed and tucked me into a fluffy, warm blanket.

"Good-night, dear," she said. She leaned over and kissed my forehead.

161

Something inside me crumbled, and I burst into tears and threw my arms around her.

She sat on the bed and held me tenderly while I hung onto her for dear life. I had been used to rough treatment all my life. Tonight, for the first time in my life, two people had said, "We love you." Someone had tucked me gently into bed like a small child and kissed me goodnight. Someone had worried about me and was angry because I had been hurt. Two people had taken me into their home and gently wiped the blood off my back and bandaged my wounds. Now they wanted me to stay here so they could protect me. It was true, they did love me! At last, someone finally did love me! I sobbed and hung onto her while she brushed back my hair and gently rocked me back and forth and spoke soothing words as if she were talking to a small child.

"It will be all right," she had said. "Everything will be all right. We love you and God loves you, too. You aren't alone. You're safe."

I wanted her to say it a thousand times—I was safe, I wasn't alone—

Finally I fell asleep in her arms. When I woke up for a few minutes during the night, I found myself lying on my side with a pillow placed next to me so I wouldn't roll over and hurt my back.

"Oh, Cloud, I wish you were here. You would never have let Flint beat me." I whispered and fell back to sleep.

The next few days were the happiest I could remember in my life. For the first time someone was giving me all the tender care I had never had as a child. Audrey was fast becoming the mother I never had and Reverend McPherson was taking the place of the father I had never known. There was peace and love in this house, and I was accepted as a member of the family.

One evening after dinner, we were sitting in the living room watching television when an old western movie came on. Practically the first scene showed the cavalry shooting down Indians.

"Why is it when the Indians are killed it's called a battle, but when the Indians kill a white man it is called a massacre?" I frowned.

"You are still fighting a war that ended a hundred years ago," Reverend McPherson said. "Stop fighting, Crying Wind. The war is over. The real war you are fighting is not in the battlefield; it is in your heart."

I would have liked to have stayed with the McPhersons forever, but I knew I had to go back home sometime. I decided I might as well get it over with. I had already been here a week.

After I moved back, I kept a constant lookout for Flint. I imagined him lurking behind every bush and watching me from every corner. After two weeks passed I relaxed. Maybe Flint wasn't even here anymore. Maybe he had gone to Mexico where there were still many of the Kickapoo.

On my way home from church one night, he was waiting for me.

"You've been to church again, haven't you?" he said as he walked slowly toward me.

"Yes," I said, feeling strangely brave.

"If you don't give it up—" his voice dropped to a threat, "we'll sing your death chant."

My breath was taken away. "I don't believe it," I said, but I knew it was too serious for him to say unless he meant it. It was the worst thing the family could do to me. The family would have a meeting, and they would sing my death chant. No one would ever speak to me again. As far as they would be concerned, I would really be dead. All ties would be cut off forever.

"Dead?" I whispered. I almost felt dead when I said it.

"You have until Saturday to clear your mind and know who you are, to make your choice." For an instant he was my uncle again, and his voice was softer, "Come back, this new stuff you're mixed up in isn't worth losing your family over. We're all you've got."

My heart hurt, and I felt tired. I didn't want to think about this. I didn't want to make a decision. Why couldn't I just keep on like I had been? Why couldn't I go to Indian ceremonials when I felt like it and go to church when I wanted? I shouldn't have to make a choice between them. After all, wasn't I half Indian and half white. I had one foot in each world. Didn't that give me the right to go back and forth between them?

I couldn't have my family turning their backs on me forever, erasing me from their lives like the wind blows away footprints, gone as if I had never existed. No, this Jesus man wasn't worth that, He couldn't expect a person to give up his family for Him. I could remember Reverend McPherson saying something about anyone who wanted to follow Jesus had to love Him more than his own father, or mother, or wife or children, or anyone—no, Jesus wanted too much from a person. I wouldn't follow Him.

I didn't see Flint again. I had no way of knowing whether he carried out his threat or not. For the first time, I was glad Cloud wasn't here. If Flint did go ahead with his threat, I didn't like to think of Cloud going along with it. I didn't want to hear Cloud sing my death chant.

Chapter Thirteen

I decided what I needed was to talk to the wind. It was that wild goose chase he had sent me on that had caused all the trouble. He was angry with me, so he had withdrawn his favors and was going to make my life miserable until I got back on his good side again.

I decided that as soon as it was dark tonight, I would go out and seek the wind.

I waited anxiously for the sun to set. I started walking to a rocky hill on the outskirts of town. It seemed to take a long time. I felt like giving up, but I knew if the wind was angry with me, he would be sure to punish me until I was back in line.

At last I reached the little hill and climbed it. It wasn't a big hill like the one back home, and it didn't have the sacred circle of rocks on top. I didn't have much hope of the wind hearing my prayer, but I went through all the motions and called his name. Then I waited and waited for a sign that he heard me and would answer me, but there was no wind blowing, not even a faint breeze. Not even a leaf rustled, all was still. Was the wind so angry he refused to speak to me, or was it that the wind had stayed behind on the reservation? Was he out blowing across the hills and valleys, talking to other Indians? I used to think the wind could be everywhere, but he wasn't here, not tonight, not when I needed him. I remembered what Reverend McPherson had said about his God, that He was everywhere all the time. It would be nice to have a God like that.

After a while I knew the wind was not going to speak tonight, so I gave up and started the long walk back home.

I was more tired than I could ever remember being in my life, but I knew even after I went to bed there would be no rest for me. There was never any rest for me. Kickapoo—he who moves about—standing here and then there—moving, searching. That was the way of the Kickapoo. I walked past my apartment and on toward the church. As I got closer, I walked faster. I was less tired now. My heart seemed to beat faster, I felt in a hurry. Something important was about to happen, and I couldn't be late! I was nearly running now, even though an hour ago my feet had been dragging.

I ran up the steps to the church and burst through the door. Reverend McPherson was standing at the rear of the church listening to the choir practice. He turned and saw me hurrying toward him.

"Crying Wind!" He seemed to sense that this was not an ordinary visit.

"I went to talk to the wind—he wasn't there. He didn't answer. I want a god who is always there; who always answers. Whenever I try to talk to the old gods, your new God keeps getting in the way. Your God is always coming into my thoughts, and I don't even know who He is!"

"I think you know who God is. I think you've always known in your heart. That's the reason you were always so restless, why you had so many doubts and questions. God kept calling to you, but you wouldn't answer Him."

"Why can't He just leave me alone!" I rebelled one last time.

"Because God loves you too much to just leave you alone! He cares about you. He loves you, and He won't give up on you just because you are stubborn. There is no place you can go to escape God's love. He has called your name, Crying Wind. He wants you to follow Him. He wants you to accept His love."

I stood on the threshold, uncertain. Then I heard the choir singing the words of a hymn and its message touched my heart,

O Love that wilt not let me go,
I rest my weary soul in Thee.

It was like the gentle flutter of a butterfly's wings in my heart. A quiet stirring, almost so soft that it went unnoticed, but I had felt it. I knew it was there.

God loved me! Whether I was good or bad, I didn't have to be anyone special or important, He loved me just the way I was right this very minute.

O Love that wilt not let me go,
I rest my weary soul in Thee.

Yes that was me! My soul was weary from searching, it longed for rest. Yes, God loved me too much to leave me alone. He had protected me as a child. He had saved me from taking my own life, He had led me to this church and the McPhersons. He had allowed Grandmother's house to be burned down so I would be forced to live here in the city where I would learn about Him. I could see so much now—so many things leading me, guiding me right up to this very moment.

"Do you want to pray?" Reverend McPherson asked in a quiet voice.

"I don't know what to say."

"Say whatever is in your heart."

"God—God—God, can You hear me? Do You know who I am? I'm Crying Wind. I used to belong to the wind, but now I belong to You—if You want me."

And then the tears came. I kept talking and crying, but I can't remember what I said. Time had no meaning as I talked to God for the first time. It was almost too much to accept all at once. God loved me—*me—me!* Jesus died for me—me! Now I was saved. I was a Christian, a child of God! I looked over at Reverend McPherson. He was smiling and wiping his eyes with his handkerchief.

"God, can You hear me? I'm Crying Wind. I used to belong to the wind, but now I belong to You—if You want me."

"Praise God," he said quietly. "Praise His holy name. At this very moment the name of Crying Wind is echoing throughout heaven. Audrey and I have prayed for you so many times. Now our prayer has been answered. God has something great and wonderful planned for your life. You were such a rebel. He worked so hard to claim your soul that He will have work for you to do."

"I wonder what my future holds now," I said, feeling, for the first time in my life, that I really had a future.

"I don't know what the future holds, but I know who holds the future," he said.

We talked awhile longer, and then he left me inside the

church while he went after Audrey. They drove me home. There was a new richness in our friendship now—now I was truly a member of their family. A few hours ago I had had nothing; now I had everything.

I went inside the apartment and knew it was different. I didn't live here alone anymore, Jesus lived here with me. I would never be alone again!

I read the Bible until I couldn't hold my eyes open any longer. I lay in bed, thinking about Grandmother and wishing I could have told her about Jesus. Then I thought about my mother and father and found no bitterness in my heart for them. There was no anger left in me. The burning war fires had been quenched and would never be lit again. This was good. My weary, restless soul had at last found peace and rest.

I fell asleep and slept like an infant in its mother's arms. When I awoke the next morning, the world was fresh and new, and so was I. The sun was bright, and life had never seemed so good. I found myself smiling all the time and singing Christmas carols, because they were the only hymns to which I knew the words.

I began looking for a job. I wanted to work now. I wanted to stay here, close to my church and my new friends. I spent the morning looking for a job with no luck at all. At noon I stopped at a small cafe to get a sandwich and a cool drink and to rest. While I was eating my lunch, I noticed a man staring at me. Everytime I would look up, he would be watching me. Just as I was about to leave, he got up from his table and came over to me.

"Excuse me, miss, I know I've been staring and I apologize, but I was admiring your beautiful beadwork necklace. I was wondering where you bought it."

"I made it myself," I said.

"Did you really? It's lovely. I have a jewelry store a block from here. I sell Indian jewelry, mostly Navajo silver and turquoise, but other kinds, too. It's seldom you see good beadwork these days." He looked at my necklace again. "I don't suppose you have some to sell?"

"Well, I do have a couple of necklaces—" I said, my hopes rising.

"Do you think you could bring them by my shop so I could have a look at your work?" he asked and reached inside his pocket and handed me a business card.

"Yes. Do you think you might buy them?" I asked. "I used to sell beadwork to the trader."

"If your other work is as nice as this, I'm sure I'll want to buy it." He smiled and turned to walk away. Suddenly he stopped and came back.

"I just had a thought—it just occurred to me," he chuckled. "I don't suppose you would be needing employment?"

My mouth dropped open, "Why yes, that's what I'm doing today, looking for work."

"You know, this is the strangest thing. My wife and I run the jewelry shop. Besides the jewelry, we sell Indian paintings and Navajo rugs. Well, I've been trying for months to get an Indian silversmith to work for us, but we never seemed to find anyone. Our idea was that he could help wait on customers, and when business was slow, he could make jewelry. A moment ago I thought, 'Instead of a Navajo silversmith, why not an Indian girl doing beadwork?' " He stopped to catch his breath. "Why don't you come and talk to my wife? She can tell you all about the job."

I was too excited to speak, so I just followed him to his store.

During the next hour his wife showed me around the store and told me what I would have to do. It was a miracle! I would be selling things I loved and understood instead of pots and pans and china. I would be selling beautiful Indian rugs and jewelry. When business was slow, I would do beadwork, and it would be sold for me right here in the store. This time, people wanted to hire me because I was an Indian and not in spite of it! They seemed to be happy to give me the job, and I was happy to take it. It was perfect. I agreed to start the next morning. As soon as I left their store I called Reverend McPherson and Audrey.

"Do you want to hear about a miracle?" I asked. I told them what God had done for me on the very first day I was a Christian.

That night I went to church. It was a small, informal prayer meeting and afterward many of the people stayed behind to visit.

Sally was there, and I told her the good news and that I would be joining the church soon. She was overjoyed.

A lady beside us said, "We are happy to have you join our church, but it's a pity to turn your back on your culture and your heritage. I always thought the Indians were 'children of nature' and that the Indian religion was beautiful. After all, haven't you always worshiped the great spirit? Isn't he the same as God?"

I squirmed in my chair, I wanted to speak, but I was afraid. Then I saw Audrey and Sally and Reverend McPherson giving me encouraging smiles, and I found the courage to speak.

"The Indian religion is only beautiful to outsiders. To those of us who know the terror, hopelesness, and fear, it is not beautiful. I remember a young man who lost his bride, and he went to a medicine man for help. I remember him running through the night, screaming and terrified. No one ever saw him again. If the Indian religion is beautiful, why do more Indians commit suicide than any other race of people? Why are there more Indian alcoholics? The great spirit I called to was not the true God. People say it does not matter what name you call God, but it does matter or God wouldn't have said, 'Neither is there salvation in any other; for there is none other name under heaven given among men whereby we must be saved.' " I looked around. Everyone was watching me. I had said too much.

171

"Couldn't the Indians have a church and use their symbols?"

The lady spoke again. "But isn't there any way to save the Indian culture by incorporating it into Christianity? Couldn't the Indians have a church and use their symbols and change their legends into Bible truths? Don't you think that would help more of them feel at home with Christianity?"

"No, I think that would be a mistake. I cannot see peyote beadwork without thinking of the drug peyote that it represents. I cannot think about Indian legends or symbols without thinking of the past. People must be willing to turn their back on the past and change to be Christians. The symbols and beadwork of the old way are not just decorations, they represent false gods. The Indian will have to be willing to give up something. God gave up His Son. Heritage is important, but not more important than salvation. Preserving the past is important, but not more important than where you will spend eternity."

"Yes, I can see you are right," she said. "I didn't really understand before. Could you come and talk to the Women's Missionary Circle and tell them what you've just told me?"

"Oh, I couldn't do that. I could never speak in front of anyone," I said.

"You just did," said Sally, "and you did a beautiful job. If you would teach us about your people, maybe we could do more to help them."

I agreed to talk to the Missionary Circle next Thursday evening. A chance to help my people!

I went to bed that night a happy person. It seemed that until now my life had been a dried up bud on a dying vine. Then someone had poured life-giving water on me, and I was bursting into bloom.

I didn't know how I had had the courage to speak up at church, but I was sure the words had been God's.

"Thank You, Jesus," I prayed. "Thank You, Friend."

Chapter Fourteen

Mr. and Mrs. Megel were easy to work for, and I really liked my job. Nothing could have been better. Each morning I woke up happy and eager to start the day. I was always anxious to get to work. I looked forward to seeing the customers and showing them the beautiful work the Indians could do. Sometimes if a customer seemed interested, I would tell them a legend or give them information about one of the tribes that made the rugs or jewelry. They seemed to enjoy it. My life was full. I never missed church. Often Sally or one of the other church members would come by the apartment and visit me.

I didn't see Flint anymore. After that last night, he had disappeared. I called his apartment but they said he had moved, and they didn't know where. I missed Flint. I knew he was sorry for the things he had done and said, and I wanted to tell him I wasn't angry and that I understood and I had forgiven him.

I thought about Cloud a lot, and wished I knew where he was. He had been gone over a year now. I had kept hoping he would come back or get in touch with me, but as time passed, it seemed less likely that I would hear from him again. Maybe he was dead. I hoped not; I didn't want him to be dead. I wanted to tell him about Jesus and about the changes in my life. Oh, Cloud, why did you have to go away?

One day when I got home from work, I saw a letter in my mailbox. As soon as I saw the simple, round writing, I knew it was from Cloud. The return address on the envelope said he was in Oregon. I was so excited that when I ripped it open, I tore off a corner of the letter.

Cloud had found Christ, too!

The letter read:

Dear Cry,

I hope you are all right and will forgive me for walking out and leaving you alone. I had to write and tell you about something that has happened to me. After I left you I just wandered around for a long time and I ended up here in Oregon. I met a girl. She was so beautiful and so good. Well, she kept telling me about this man named Jesus. At first I didn't listen to her, but she kept telling me I needed to give my heart to this Jesus and then one day I knew she was right. I can't write the words that I want to make you understand, but the old religion is all lies. It is wrong. There is only one God. Cry, there is so much I want to tell you. Mary, this girl, and I are going to get married this summer. I found everything I was ever looking for. I even have a good job here. I work at a sportsmen's lodge and teach men how to hunt and fish. I am a guide, too. My life is good and I am happy. I want to share this happiness with you, Cry. I am sending you a book called the Bible. Please read it. Do it for me. Do you know where Flint is? Please write and tell me how you are.

Love, Cloud

I held the letter against my heart, and tears of joy ran down my cheeks. Cloud had found Jesus Christ, too! It was a miracle! We had been looking, searching for something, and we had gone in opposite directions. Then, almost at the same time, hundreds of miles apart, we had both found God!

175

I sat down to answer Cloud's letter right away and tell him the story of my own special miracle. I could see his face smiling as he would read my letter. For hundreds of years there hadn't been one single Christian in our family. Now in a matter of weeks, there were two of us!

We had nice long talks, but both of us carefully avoided mentioning the church or our fight.

Chapter Fifteen

"INDIANS TAKE OVER WOUNDED KNEE, SOUTH DAKOTA." The newspaper headlines were frightening in that early spring of 1973.

A handful of Indians, armed with old hunting rifles, had declared war against the United States. I was afraid for them. This small band of Indians was standing up against the strongest nation in the world, a nation with a multi-billion dollar defense system, millions of soldiers, tanks, missiles, bombs—surely the Indians would be wiped out and destroyed by the government. What chance did they have? Hadn't the government always killed Indians? The Indians could only lose, just as they had always lost.

Each day I scanned the papers and expected to read of the second Wounded Knee Massacre, but I never did. Days turned into weeks and the tension mounted, but still the handful of Indians held their ground.

Some AIM (American Indian Movement) members had occupied Wounded Knee to get the attention of the American people and wake them up to the poor treatment of the red man. Years of treaties and peaceful negotiations had gained them nothing. Now many Indians felt it was time for drastic measures.

Many Indians were fired up with old hatred and a strong desire to dig up the old, half-buried hatchet. Who knew how many other Indians in the country felt that way? How many would get into cars and drive to Wounded Knee, looking for revenge? Dozens? Hundreds? This generation of Indians was tired of reservation life, tired of corrupt agents, and fed up with the BIA (Bureau of Indian Affairs). They wanted changes, and they wanted changes now. That's how AIM got started, and right or wrong, it was at least getting people to take notice of the Indians.

I hadn't seen or heard from Flint, and I wondered if he was in South Dakota. I knew he would want to be in on this. He wanted to be a warrior. I had heard him cry "Indian Power!" and pretend to shoot an arrow from an imaginary bow. I had heard my uncles give the war cries that meant "It's a good day to die!"

I went to church early so I could talk to Reverend McPherson before the Wednesday evening service started. "I am confused about my feelings," I said. "I am proud of the Indians at Wounded Knee. At the same time, I am afraid for them. I even find myself wishing I were there to help them fight. I know they will be killed. The government always kills Indians. That's the way the story always ends." I felt miserable.

"I can't pretend to understand all your feelings about this," Reverend McPherson answered, "but I know how tragic it would be for anyone to die. You must remember that this isn't 1890. The cavalry isn't charging in and slaughtering helpless women and children in a bloodbath. The very fact that the government hasn't taken drastic action shows things have changed. The government is trying for a peaceful settlement."

"Why do I feel so angry?" I asked. "I'm a Christian now. I have changed my heart. Why do I feel old blood boiling up until I want to run up there and fight and scream and say, 'Look at us! We are brave! We will die for our cause!'"

He smiled. "First of all, even Christians get angry. Being angry is human, and I would say that the Indians have a right to be angry and discouraged and frustrated. I don't think you should grab a spear and go charging off, but there are other things you could do to help."

"How can anyone help a lost cause?" I mumbled.

178

"No cause is lost as long as someone believes deeply in it. The first thing to do is pray."

I looked up.

"We can pray for the Indians to use sound judgment; we can pray for the government to be reasonable and just; and we can pray for God's guidance for all those involved. After that, we can write letters to other churches, to senators, and to anyone we can think of who can help." His voice showed his enthusiasm. "You can help your people, Crying Wind, but haven't you heard that the pen is mightier than the sword?"

"Or spear?" I smiled.

As the prayer service started, I expected the usual requests for people in the hospital or people who were having problems. Instead, Reverend McPherson called for a special prayer service for those involved at Wounded Knee. My eyes filled with tears as one person after another came to the altar and prayed for a handful of Indians they didn't know and probably didn't agree with. I knew there had been no prayer service for the Indians in 1890. Times were changing. People did care, but they had to be told what was happening. There was such a lump in my throat that my own prayer had to be silent, but I prayed; "Please, God, don't let anyone get killed. Let me help if I can, and please, don't let Flint be up there. But if he is, take care of him."

Weeks passed. I began to wonder if it would ever end, but it finally did. A Methodist minister helped make the arrangements to bring a close to Wounded Knee.

I let out a big sigh of relief. The government hadn't killed all the Indians. Things really were changing!

My phone rang early one morning and woke me up.

"Hello," I said sleepily.

"Is this Crying Wind?" A strange voice asked.

"Yes." I waited.

"Are you related to a man named Flint Pakotah?"

179

"Yes, he is my uncle." I was beginning to feel afraid.

"We found your name and phone number in his billfold. He has been injured in a highway traffic accident. He has been taken to Memorial Hospital."

"I'll come right away," I said, and hung up, still not knowing who had called.

I arrived at the hospital and asked to see Flint. I was told to wait until his doctor could talk to me.

It was nearly an hour before a man in a long white coat came and sat down beside me and told me about Flint. He had been driving fast, too fast, and had missed a corner. His truck had rolled down a steep hill and crashed at the bottom. Luckily, someone had seen the accident and reported it, and an ambulance brought him here. He was banged up pretty badly. He had three broken ribs and a broken leg, but he was lucky to be alive. I wanted to see him, but the doctor told me he was asleep and I should come back the next day.

When I returned the next afternoon and walked into his room, I was unprepared for how bad he looked. His eyes were black and nearly swollen shut, there was a bandage across his nose and another on his forehead. There was tape across his chest, his left leg was up in a sling, and he seemed to have bruises on every inch of his body.

"Hi, Flint," I said and eased over toward the bed.

He pressed his lips together and shut his eyes.

"Do you hurt bad?" I asked, knowing he would never admit to feeling pain.

He wouldn't answer.

My spirits sank. He had gone ahead with my death chant, as far as he was concerned I was dead.

"Can I do anything?"

No answer.

I stood there a minute and decided I might as well leave. As

180

I left, I told him, "If you need anything, have someone call me. I'm sorry you were hurt."

I told myself there was no point in wasting my time. He would never speak to me. I would not go back and see him.

But try as I might, I couldn't get him out of my mind, so the next day I went back to see him. Again he refused to speak to me. I left and was determined I wouldn't go back again. I held out for a week, but I couldn't stay away any longer.

"Hi Flint." I tried to sound cheerful.

He was silent. I was getting ready to leave when suddenly he said, "What are you doing here?"

I was so relieved to have him speak to me at last!

"I wanted to see how you are doing." I walked closer. "You don't look too good."

"How did you know I was here?" he asked, but avoided my eyes.

"Someone found your wallet. My phone number was in it."

More silence between us.

"What happened?" I asked.

"I was coming back from a peyote ceremony—" he looked up at the ceiling, "I thought I saw a huge eagle coming at me, and I swerved to miss him—there was no eagle."

"Peyote!" I shook my head. "It will kill you."

"Why don't you get out of here?" he snapped and closed his eyes.

I left without saying anymore.

The next day I had a head cold and felt so bad I didn't even go to work. It was several more days before I felt well enough to try to see Flint again.

This time when I walked into his room, Flint raised up and looked at me.

"I didn't think you would be back," he said.

I shrugged my shoulders, "I care about you."

181

He looked at the cast on his leg and then said quietly, "I'm glad you came. I'm sorry about what I did, Cry."

I had never heard Flint say he was sorry for anything he had ever done in his life.

"Forget it." I quickly changed the subject. "How are you feeling?"

"Rotten. I hate being tied up here like an animal."

"When can you leave?"

"Not for a couple of weeks, she says."

"She says?" I asked. "I thought your doctor was a man."

Flint looked embarrassed. "He is. I meant one of the nurses told me it would be a couple of weeks."

"Are they taking care of you? Do you need anything?"

"I'm OK. She brought me some books and loaned me this little battery radio to listen to." He nodded toward a small radio beside his bed.

"She?" I asked.

"One of the nurses," he said, and this time he changed the subject.

Now that he was talking to me, I visited him every day after work. His leg was healing, and his ribs were better. He was looking like himself again, but he wasn't acting like himself. He seemed more lighthearted, and he smiled and joked more than he ever had.

One day while we were talking, he asked, "Cry, do you remember the story your grandmother used to tell about why the Kickapoo hate the Pawnee?"

I had to think for a moment. "Yes, I remember."

"Tell it to me, I've forgotten."

"The Kickapoo and Pawnee have always been enemies. The Pawnee were sneaky and they were afraid of Kickapoo warriors. The Pawnee would wait until the Kickapoo warriors went hunting, and then the Pawnee would attack the women and old people left behind in the camps. In the hot summer of 1845, some Pawnee stole horses from a Kickapoo hunting party at Little River. The Kickapoo were so angry they chased the Pawnee, ran them down, and killed them all. The Kickapoo took back not only their own horses, but all the Pawnee horses, too." I could hear Grandmother's voice telling the story. "The Kickapoo made a vow then and there to seek vengeance on the Pawnee from that time on. To seal their vow, they cut off the arm of one of the Pawnee braves and sent it back to the Pawnee as a warning."

"That was 130 years ago." Flint sighed, "A long time ago. A long time to be angry."

"What do you mean?"

"Oh, nothing, I guess. There is a nurse here. She is Pawnee. I knew the Kickapoo hated the Pawnee, but I couldn't remember why. Now I know it is because of horses stolen 130 years ago." He laughed. "I will have to tell her that."

I couldn't help but notice he spoke more and more often of "that nurse."

"What is her name?"

My question caught him by surprise. "Oh, I don't know, I forget. Autumn Rose, I think."

"That's a beautiful name," I said. "Is she as beautiful as her name?"

"I didn't notice. She's just a nurse." He began to talk about the weather.

I wanted to tell Flint that I had heard from Cloud, but if I did he was sure to ask what Cloud said. Then I would have to tell him about Cloud becoming a Christian, and about myself, too. I knew he wasn't ready to talk about that, so I kept it in my heart and saved it for another time.

Flint was getting stronger and looking better each day. He now welcomed my visits. We had nice long talks, but both of us

I smiled and began. "You see, there was this man named Jesus."

carefully avoided mentioning the church or our fight because neither of us wanted to cause trouble between us.

One night when I entered his room I knew right away something was wrong by the angry look on his face. "What's wrong?" I asked. I saw his untouched dinner tray beside his bed.

"Nothing," he said in a tone of voice that meant something was very wrong.

"Are you worse?"

"No. I'm OK."

"I can see that you aren't."

"Oh, it's nothing. It's not important," he said.

"Flint?" I pushed on trying to find out what it was.

"I found out I would be getting out of here soon and, well—I asked that nurse if I could call on her after I got out of the hospital."

184

Before I could speak the door opened and a nurse came in and picked up his tray.

"You should have tried to eat something. Perhaps you'll feel like eating later," she said cheerfully and went out the door with the tray.

"That was her," he whispered, in case she was still within hearing distance.

I couldn't believe it! Flint had fallen for a girl, and a Pawnee girl at that!

He shrugged his shoulders. "Nothing to worry about anyway. She won't go out with me." He tried to look as if he didn't care, but I could see in his face that he was hurt by her refusal.

"Why not? Because you are Kickapoo?"

"The truth is—" He swallowed hard and turned his face away from me. "The truth is—I asked her out and she asked me if I was a Christian."

"What!" I walked around to the other side of the bed so I could see him.

"She asked me if I was a Christian." He shook his head. "I said to her, 'what kind of a question is that?' She said she was a Christian and didn't date men who weren't Christians."

I stood there in silence trying to think of something to say that might help. Flint must really think she was something special to be so miserable about being turned down by her.

Before we could talk any more, the bell went off to end visiting hours. I promised to be back tomorrow and then I left.

At the end of the hall I could see the nurse Flint was talking about. She was waiting for an elevator and I walked up and stood beside her.

I wondered what it was about her that Flint thought was so special. She was short and a little overweight, her dark brown eyes looked like the eyes of a fawn, and her black hair was cut very short. She was a Pawnee. A year or even a month ago

Flint wouldn't have considered speaking to a Pawnee, and here he was now longing to court a Pawnee girl. He was changing, just a little, but he was changing.

She saw me watching her and she smiled. When I saw her smile I knew that was what had captured Flint. In her smile was all the warmth and gentleness of a summer day.

I smiled back and then I noticed something else about her. Around her neck on a small gold chain was a tiny gold cross. I knew it was that cross and what it meant to her that kept her from going out with my uncle.

"You are Flint's niece, aren't you?" she asked. "He told me you were coming to visit him."

I nodded. "Yes, he is my uncle. I am worried about him. Will he be all right?"

"Yes. He can probably leave the hospital next week," she said. There was a long pause of silence.

"He likes you," I said boldly.

She lowered her eyes and said shyly, "I like him, too." Her fingers moved upward and gently touched the little cross on her necklace, "If only—" she stopped.

The elevator arrived and the doors opened, and she stepped inside.

"Up or down?" she said.

"Neither. I forgot something. I have to go back and see Flint a few minutes," I said.

"Maybe I'll see you again," she said, and she let the elevator door close.

I had a feeling we would be seeing a lot of each other.

I walked back to Flint's room.

He was surprised to see me back again.

I pulled up a chair beside his bed and put my hand on his arm.

"Flint, my uncle." I took a deep breath. "Cloud and I have a story we want to share with you—"

187

He looked at me with a deep, lonely hunger in his eyes.

I smiled and began. "You see, there was this man named Jesus—"